weber's

fresh on the grill ™

weber's

fresh on the grill™

flavours of the mediterranean

matthew drennan

Published by MQ Publications Limited
12 The Ivories
6-8 Northampton Street
London N1 2HY
Tel: +44 (0)20 7359 2244
Fax: +44 (0)20 7359 1616
email: mail@mqpublications.com
website: www.mqpublications.com

Editorial team:
Managing Editor: Ljiljana Ortolja-Baird
Editors: Kate John, Abi Rowsell and Marsha Capen
Recipe photography: Ken Field
Food Styling: Matthew Drennan, Debbie Major and Carol Tennant
Styling: Angela Swaffield
Illustrations: Marc Dando
Book design concept: Balley Design Associates
Page layout: Yvonne Dedman
Recipe credits: Matthew Drennan

Produced by:
MQ Publications Ltd. under exclusive licence from
Weber-Stephen Products Co.

MQ Publications:
Zaro Weil, CEO & Publisher

Weber-Stephen Products Co.:
Mike Kempster Sr., Executive Vice President;
Jeff Stephen, Vice President Export Sales;
Marsha Capen, Director of Marketing

1 3 5 7 9 8 6 4 2

A CIP catalogue record for this book is available
from the British Library

ISBN: 1 84072 355 6

Printed in France

Contents

foreword

As I flip through the pages of this beautiful book, it amazes me how far Weber grilling has come. In 1952 who would have guessed that the covered grill that my father, George Stephen, was building for my family's backyard in Midwestern America would one day cross the Atlantic and find a natural place in the cooking of Europe?

In some ways it makes perfect sense. My father landed on a sensational idea – a solution really, to the flaws of the open grills so common in his day. His domed kettle simply made food taste better, cooking it faster, more evenly and always with a distinctive touch of smokiness. With a clever design and reliable parts, my dad launched the company that would make America's most beloved grills and inspire a tradition of year-round outdoor grilling.

It's no accident that Europeans recognise Weber® grills for the same qualities. After all, this is a place where the pursuit of great cooking and great food is a way of life. The recipes and techniques in this book illustrate that dozens of dishes from Europe's exciting cooking styles reach new heights on the sizzling grates of covered grills.

All of us at Weber are proud that our family-owned company has travelled so far and wide. Although my father is no longer with us, I think his legacy lives on every time you cook a meal outside on the grill and enjoy it leisurely with family and friends. Dad loved a barbecue anytime of the year, whether it was for an everyday event or a special occasion. I am sure he would join me in wishing you all the fun and flavour that grilling provides.

Here's to more good times!

Jeff Stephen

Jeff Stephen
Vice President Export Sales
Weber-Stephen Products Co.

introduction

Mediterranean cooking is one of the hottest topics in kitchens around the world today. Blessed with year round sunshine, clear blue waters, and an abundance of fresh produce, the Mediterranean region is a treasure-trove of nature's finest fare. Whether slow-roasted or char-grilled, cooking with these ingredients on the barbecue enhances the distinctive flavours, aromas and colours of this much-loved part of the world.

This inspired collection of more than 100 specially created recipes combines the very best of French, Italian, Spanish, Greek and Moroccan cuisine with the grilling expertise of Weber, the world's leading manufacturer of outdoor grills. With delicious fish, meat and vegetarian dishes to choose from, each bursting with fresh ingredients such as tomatoes sun-ripened on the vine, pungent green olives, sweet peppers and fragrant figs and lemons, this beautiful book is both a visual feast and a tantalising taste of the Mediterranean.

Our culinary journey through this sun-drenched region begins with a look inside the Mediterranean store-cupboard, revealing staple ingredients such as olive oil, tomato purée, vinegars and seasonings. The native cuisine is rich in aromatic herbs and spices and this opening chapter presents a wide range of recipes for relishes, piquant sauces, spice rubs, dressings, and butters flavoured with saffron and rosemary. From Moroccan Chilli Sauce to Greek Lemon and Oregano Marinade or classic Italian Pesto, they will bring the flavours of the sun to any dish.

While Mediterranean has become a general term used to describe a diverse area that encompasses many styles and cultures, its name rightly belongs to the vast stretch of water that flows through the Strait of Gibraltar. Defining the coastlines of southern Europe and northern Africa, it brings with it a tide of plenty in the form of fresh fish and shellfish, an essential part of the local diet and economy. The second section of this book features a wide variety of recipes that bring to life the quaint fishing ports of Greece and southern Spain, and range from extravagant Lobster Greek Style to quick and easy Swordfish Kebabs and Bay Leaves.

Poultry and meat also play an important part in Mediterranean cookery and are perfect for barbecue cooking. Irresistible recipes using a variety of

different cuts are included, from Moroccan Ginger-Marinated Chicken with Sweet Tomato Jam, to a hearty Italian Rack of Venison with Garlic and Rosemary or Middle Eastern influenced Coriander Spiced Lamb Fillets with Lemon Tahini Sauce.

Mediterranean meals would not be complete without fresh vegetables and salads, and family dinners often feature a multitude of small dishes that use a delicious array of home-grown produce. A selection of tasty dips, risottos, salads and accompaniments include Red Pepper, Aubergine and Coriander Dip served with pitta bread, Artichokes with Goat Cheese and Sweet Basil Dressing, Tomato and Tapenade Peppers with Pistou and Provençal-style warm salads.

Throughout the book step-by-step illustrations help to guide you through the more complicated cookery techniques such as jointing a chicken or preparing a lobster for the grill, and there is information on cooking with indigenous ingredients such as chillies, polenta and mozzarella. With clear instructions and easy-to-follow recipes you will soon master an extensive repertoire of barbecuing skills and dishes.

The final chapter contains guidance for successful barbecuing from Weber. It includes advice on Direct and Indirect cooking methods, using charcoal and gas barbecues and tips on cleaning and the maintenance of your barbecue. There is also a section giving essential safety information, advice on the right tools for the best results and an explanation of optimum cooking times.

With the help of these authentic recipes, inspirational photographs and insights into local ingredients and cooking styles, you really can bring the flavours of the Mediterranean into your own kitchen. Much of the appeal of Mediterranean-style eating lies in its use of simple yet delicious ingredients and in cultivating a relaxed, fun attitude to dining, and this more than anything is at the very heart of barbecue culture.

flavours of the sun

The store cupboard

Whatever fresh meat, poultry, fish or vegetables you opt to barbecue, the store cupboard will play an important supporting role, as you draw on its selection of oils, vinegars, herbs, spices and various bottled and canned flavourings and ingredients. Featured here is a fine selection, which covers both the essential and the exciting.

Oils

Olive oil: Olive varieties vary all over the Mediterranean, so quality and flavour of oil will differ from country to country. A bottle will state the grade of oil, level of acidity, country of origin and the producer's name. Supermarket brands are cheaper, but are often of mediocre quality – using olive oils from different countries and blending them. Single-estate oils are of the best quality.

• **Italian** oils, especially those from the Tuscany region, are among the finest in the world. Italian oils are usually deep green in colour, with a pronounced peppery after-taste.

• **Spanish** olive oil is a deep golden-yellow with a lighter, fresher flavour and a slightly peppery taste.

• **Greek** oils are very good value and have a similar green colour to the Italian oils, but tend to lack their intense flavour.

• **France** produces fewer oils than other countries, but they are fine oils, pale in colour and light in flavour.

Extra virgin olive oil: This is the first clear premium oil that is pressed and extracted from the olives. The quality is determined by its acidity, the higher the acidity the lower the quality. Extra virgin must have an acidity of less than one per cent. This expensive oil is best used as a flavouring in its own right. Whisk it into dressings or pour directly over barbecued fish or vegetables. Avoid using it in dishes that require high temperatures.

Vegetable oil: The most common vegetable oils are sunflower, corn and groundnut. Lacking in taste they are however good for brushing over most foods for barbecuing, to help avoid the food sticking to the cooking grate, without altering the flavour.

Vinegars

Red and white wine vinegar: These are mainly used in marinades and dressings, especially if a fresh lemon is not to hand. The acidity they give is used to help flavours penetrate meat, poultry and fish. They are also vital to many flavoured dressings, to help cut through the heavy olive oil.

Balsamic vinegar: This is hardly a staple of the store cupboard, but definitely a barbecue cook's treat. The famous dark vinegar is made only in and around the region of Modena in northern Italy. It has a wonderful mellow sweet-sour flavour that is fantastic with the smokiness of barbecued foods. While expensive, a little splash goes a long way.

Seasonings

Salt: An essential ingredient in the kitchen and the amount required in any recipe is down to the cook, hence why recipes often say 'season to taste'. Kitchen or table salt is a good all-rounder, but sea salt is particularly good for its strong taste and adds a good crunch to fresh salads or grilled vegetables.

Pepper: Once pepper is ground it quickly loses its pungent aroma, so it's always important to grind black pepper straight onto your food.

Spices

Whole spices keep better for longer than ready-ground, and the aroma and flavour of a freshly ground spice is unbeatable. The main spices that you will find throughout this book are; **whole allspice, fennel seeds, cinnamon** (sticks and ground), **coriander** (seeds and ground), **cumin** (seeds and ground) and **caraway seeds.** Whole spices (except cinnamon sticks) should be lightly toasted in a small pan over a high heat for a few minutes until their aroma is just released, then left to cool and ground using a mortar and pestle.

Saffron: This spice is either soaked in warm water to release its colour and flavour, or ground to a powder.

Crushed chillies or dried chilli flakes: These are a brilliant alternative to fresh chillies and will add a good background heat to any marinade or sauce.

Paprika: This is the ground red powder made from mild and hot red peppers.

Herbs

Herbs breathe life into most barbecue dishes, adding flavour, aroma and colour.

Fresh herbs are unbeatable and are best purchased or picked as near the preparation or cooking time as possible. **Dill**, **fennel**, **chives**, **summer thyme**, **sage**, **parsley**, **tarragon**, **oregano** and **marjoram** are best loosely wrapped in damp kitchen paper, then placed in a plastic bag and kept in the salad drawer of the refrigerator for up to three days. **Basil** however does not like the cold and is best bought in growing pots and kept watered in a cool well-lit spot in the kitchen. A few of the woody, or more robust dried herbs survive the drying process reasonably well, for example, **rosemary**, **thyme**, **sage** and **oregano**. You can use dried **bay leaves** for flavouring dishes but use fresh bay leaves for skewering on kebabs.

Flavourings

Sun-dried tomato purée: This flavourful tomato purée is a blend of sun-dried tomatoes, herbs and spices, and is a great standby for adding depth, flavour and colour to tomato-based sauces, pizzas and marinades.

Harissa: The fiery chilli paste from North Africa makes a good standby marinade. Look for speciality brands or make your own (page 21).

Dijon mustard: Its clean, sharp and mild flavour makes this mustard perfect for dressings and sauces, and the ideal partner to barbecued meats.

Honey: This is a good ingredient to have to hand for barbecue marinades and glazes.

Canned/jarred goods

Chopped tomatoes: Italian chopped tomatoes offer the best flavour for authentic sauces and pizza toppings.

Pulses: Keep a few cans of pulses to hand, to make a simple and delicious bean salad (page 179). Butter, borlotti and cannellini beans are good staples.

Anchovies: Fresh anchovies are eaten all over the Mediterranean, particularly southern Italy, but preserved anchovies in jars or cans are a convenient alternative. Essential for classics such as Pissaladière (page 52).

Tuna: Opt for tuna canned in oil, as this has a better flavour and has more nutrients. Italian brands are worth paying that little bit extra for.

Gherkins: These are great with barbecued food or to serve with drinks. The tiny pickled variety of gherkin from France, known as *cornichons*, have a sweet, nutty flavour.

Capers: Capers are the olive green buds of the caper plant native to many Mediterranean regions. They are sold pickled in brine and used to add piquancy to dressings and sauces such as Salsa verde (page 23).

Olives: All over the Mediterranean, olives are sold loose at market stalls where you can often sample before you buy. Shop around to find your favourite. Keep a can or jar of olives to hand in the store cupboard. Particular pre-packed olives to look for are Spanish green manzanilla, Greek kalamata olives, or the small black niçoise olives.

And finally...

Your store cupboard should also contain such staples as a packet or two of **rice**, **polenta**, **couscous** and a good selection of **dried pasta**. For classic Italian risotto (page 84), buy the correct rice. Look for either *arborio*, *carnaroli* or *vialone nano*. Some brands are simply sold as risotto rice. Short-grain and long-grain rice is used a lot in Spanish dishes, often flavoured and coloured with saffron as for classic paella. Polenta is a brilliant store-cupboard staple and, of course, once cooked and set is wonderful to barbecue.

Flavoured butters

Whether or not you have opted to marinate before cooking, here is another way to add a blast of flavour to barbecued food. A thick slice of flavoured butter becomes an instant sauce as it slowly melts onto hot sizzling meat, chicken, fish or vegetables, releasing its flavours as it becomes liquid. The secret lies in finely chopping or crushing your choice of flavouring before stirring them into the softened butter, then simply chill until firm or freeze for use in the future.

The flavoured butter recipes all serve 8–10.

Black olive butter

225g/8oz unsalted butter, softened
100g/4oz black olives, stoned
1 plump garlic clove, crushed
1 tablespoon fresh thyme leaves, chopped
a pinch of salt
freshly ground black pepper

Put the butter, olives, garlic, thyme and seasoning into a food processor and blend until almost smooth. Using the food processor really mashes the olives to give the butter a wonderful purple colour. Spoon the butter onto a large sheet of greaseproof paper or foil. Roll up the butter neatly inside the paper into a log shape then secure the ends like a Christmas cracker. Chill in the refrigerator to firm up. Cut into thick slices and serve on top of sizzling hot chicken, meat, fish or vegetables straight from the barbecue.

Saffron butter

225g/8oz unsalted butter, softened
large pinch of saffron strands
1 tablespoon fresh parsley, chopped
a pinch of salt
freshly ground black pepper

Beat the butter in a medium-sized bowl until softened. Crush the saffron strands to a fine powder using a mortar and pestle. Add to the softened butter and beat very well until the butter takes on the colour of the saffron. Stir in the chopped parsley and seasoning. Spoon the butter onto a large sheet of greaseproof paper or foil. Roll up the butter neatly inside the paper into a log shape, then secure the ends like a Christmas cracker. Chill in the refrigerator to firm up. Cut into thick slices and serve on top of sizzling hot fish or chicken straight from the barbecue.

Fennel butter

1 tablespoon fennel seeds
225g/8oz unsalted butter, softened
1 tablespoon thick Greek honey
1 tablespoon ouzo (Greek aniseed liqueur) or Pernod
sea salt
freshly ground black pepper

Heat a small heavy-based pan on the hob and add the fennel seeds. Continue heating gently until their aroma rises. Remove from the heat and crush roughly using a mortar and pestle. Beat the butter until softened and add the crushed fennel, honey, ouzo and seasoning. Beat well until the alcohol is amalgamated into the flavoured butter. Spoon the butter on to a large sheet of greaseproof paper or foil. Roll up the butter neatly inside the paper into a log shape then secure the ends like a Christmas cracker. Chill in the refrigerator to firm up. Cut into thick slices and serve on top of sizzling hot chicken, lamb, fish or shellfish straight from the barbecue.

Rosemary & garlic butter [pictured]

225g/8oz unsalted butter, softened
2 large plump garlic cloves
1 tablespoon fresh rosemary, finely chopped

Following the steps above, beat the butter in a large bowl until softened. Crush the garlic in a garlic crusher or chop into small pieces with a knife then mash to a paste with a little salt. **1** Add the garlic to the softened butter with the chopped rosemary and beat well. **2** Spoon the butter on to a large sheet of greaseproof paper or foil. **3** Roll up the flavoured butter neatly inside the paper into a log shape, then secure both ends like a Christmas cracker. Chill in the refrigerator to firm up. Cut the log into thick slices and serve on top of sizzling hot lamb, steaks or pork chops.

Roquefort & peppercorn butter

150g/5oz unsalted butter, softened
100g/4oz Roquefort cheese
1 tablespoon green peppercorns in brine, drained
1 tablespoon fresh chives, finely chopped
a pinch of salt
freshly ground black pepper

Put the butter and Roquefort into a food processor and blend until almost smooth. Put into a bowl and stir in the peppercorns, chives and seasoning. Spoon the butter onto a large sheet of greaseproof paper or foil. Roll up the butter neatly inside the paper into a log shape then secure the ends like a Christmas cracker. Chill in the refrigerator to firm up. Cut into thick slices and serve on top of sizzling hot chicken, pork chops, steaks or vegetables straight from the barbecue.

Marinades

Tenderising was once the major function of marinating, but since most of the meat and poultry we buy today is young and tender, we concentrate on the flavour aspect of the technique. A marinade imparts extra flavours to all varieties of food.

Starting with a base of olive oil and an acid, such as citrus juice, wine or vinegar, there is no end to the combinations of spices, herbs, fruit zest, aromatic seeds, alcohol or other flavourings you can add to concoct a unique marinade. These flavours simply need time to penetrate and develop.

Because of the acidic content of marinades, the process is best done in a non-reactive container, like a glass or glazed bowl. Slashing the skin and flesh of meat, poultry and fish will help the marinade's flavours to penetrate and accelerate the process. Meat, fish or poultry should always be left to marinate in the refrigerator. While marinated fish and poultry should be transferred directly from the refrigerator to the barbecue, meat (that is lamb, pork and beef, with the exception of ground beef), should be brought to room temperature 20 to 30 minutes before barbecuing.

The marinade recipes all serve 4.

Greek lemon & oregano marinade

(for lamb, pork, veal, chicken, fish or vegetables)

150ml/$\frac{1}{4}$ pint olive oil
1 lemon, juice and pared rind
2 tablespoons fresh oregano, roughly torn
sea salt
freshly ground black pepper

Mix all the ingredients well in a bowl, along with salt and pepper to taste. Arrange the meat, chicken, fish or vegetables in a single layer in a large shallow dish and pour over the marinade. Cover and leave to marinate in the refrigerator for about 1 hour (fish for only about 30 minutes).

Herbs de Provence marinade

(for any meat, chicken, fish or vegetables)

1 teaspoon dried fennel seeds, crushed
1 tablespoon fresh rosemary, chopped
1 tablespoon fresh sage, chopped
1 tablespoon fresh savoury, chopped
1 tablespoon fresh thyme, chopped
150ml/$\frac{1}{4}$ pint olive oil
2 tablespoons white wine vinegar
sea salt
freshly ground black pepper

Put the dried fennel seeds and the fresh herbs into a small bowl. Pour in the olive oil and vinegar, and season. Mix together well. Arrange the meat, chicken, fish or vegetables in a single layer in a large shallow dish and pour the marinade over it, making sure all the food is well coated. Cover and leave to marinate in the refrigerator for about 1 hour (fish for only about 30 minutes).

Italian balsamic marinade

(for pork, veal, chicken, fish or vegetables)

150ml/¼ pint olive oil
1 plump garlic clove, crushed
1 shallot, finely chopped
2 tablespoons fresh mint, chopped
1 teaspoon dried oregano
1 teaspoon capers, roughly chopped
2 tablespoons balsamic vinegar
freshly ground black pepper

In a small bowl, mix together the oil, garlic, shallot, mint, oregano, capers and balsamic vinegar, with pepper to taste (you don't need salt as the capers are salty). Arrange the meat, chicken, fish or vegetables in a single layer in a large shallow dish and pour the marinade over it. Cover and leave to marinate in the refrigerator for about 1 hour (fish for only about 30 minutes).

Spanish-style marinade

(for chicken, fish or vegetables)

2 plump garlic cloves
2 teaspoons fresh thyme leaves
sea salt
freshly ground black pepper
1 lemon, juice only
½ teaspoon paprika
8 tablespoons olive oil

Using a mortar and pestle, crush the garlic and herbs with a little salt and pepper until almost smooth. Put into a bowl, add the lemon juice, paprika and oil, and mix well. Arrange the chicken, fish or vegetables in a single layer in a shallow dish and pour the marinade over it. Cover and leave to marinate in the refrigerator for about 1 hour (fish for only about 30 minutes).

Moroccan chilli marinade

(for lamb, chicken, fish or vegetables)

1 teaspoon cumin seeds
large handful of fresh coriander, chopped
1 small onion, very finely chopped
1 red chilli, deseeded and finely chopped
2 plump garlic cloves, crushed
8 tablespoons olive oil
1 lemon, juice only
sea salt
freshly ground black pepper

Heat a small heavy-based pan on the hob and add the cumin seeds. Shake them around for a few seconds until their aroma rises. Remove from the heat and crush roughly using a mortar and pestle. Put the seeds into a bowl with the coriander, onion, chilli, garlic, oil and lemon juice. Add salt and pepper to taste and mix all the ingredients together well. Arrange the meat, chicken, fish or vegetables in a single layer in a large shallow dish and pour over the marinade. Cover and leave to marinate in the refrigerator for about 1 hour (fish for only about 30 minutes).

Spice rubs

A spice 'rub' is a dry version of a marinade. While most marinades are oil-based and work by letting the flavour seep into the meat or fish, the spice or herb rub is rubbed directly into the food. A splash of oil can also be added to a rub to make it more of a paste, if you prefer. As with marinades, slashing or cutting into the skin and flesh of meat, poultry and fish will help the rub's flavours to penetrate and speed up the process.

The rub recipes are for about 900g/2lb meat, poultry or fish.

Coriander & spice rub

(for lamb, chicken or fish)

½ **teaspoon saffron strands**

1 teaspoon ground cumin

½ **teaspoon ground coriander**

1 teaspoon chilli powder

1 lemon, finely grated rind only

1 garlic clove, crushed

½ **teaspoon salt**

½ **teaspoon freshly ground black pepper**

Grind the saffron to a powder using a mortar and pestle. Put all the ingredients into a small bowl and mix very well. Rub into the flesh of the fish, chicken or lamb. Cover and leave to marinate in the refrigerator for about 1 hour (fish for only about 30 minutes).

Lemon & herb rub

(for lamb, chicken or fish)

2 lemons

2 teaspoons flaked sea salt

1 teaspoon freshly ground black pepper

1 teaspoon fresh rosemary, chopped

1 teaspoon fresh thyme, chopped

Preheat the oven to 140°C/275°F/Gas 1. Using a vegetable peeler, pare off the lemon rind in big strips, making sure there is no bitter white pith attached. Put the strips of rind on a baking tray, put into an oven and roast for 15–20 minutes, until pale golden and dry. Leave to cool. Using a mortar and pestle, grind the lemon rind roughly with the salt. Stir in the pepper and chopped herbs and mix well. Use to rub into the flesh of fish, chicken or lamb. Cover and leave to marinate in the refrigerator for about 1 hour (fish for only about 30 minutes).

Sauces, relishes & chutneys

If you prefer the clean unadulterated flavour of a barbecued piece of meat or fish, then why not team it with a spoonful of a home-made relish or chutney at the table. With a wealth of ingredients from which to choose, you can create simply mouth-watering condiments, from vivid green pesto and pungent tapenade, to fiery harissa (Moroccan chilli sauce).

These recipes will serve 4 unless otherwise indicated.

Mayonnaise

Light or pure olive oil are the best choice for this recipe, as extra virgin olive oil has too overpowering a flavour.

2 egg yolks
salt
2 teaspoons Dijon mustard
150ml /^{1}/$_2$ pint olive oil
150ml /^{1}/$_2$ pint vegetable oil
1 tablespoon white wine vinegar
squeeze of lemon juice

Put the egg yolks in a food processor with a pinch of salt and the mustard and blend briefly until smooth. Stir the two oils together. With the motor still running, add half the blended oil in a slow steady trickle until the mixture is very thick. (Take your time in adding the oil, so it amalgamates and thickens the yolks.) Add the vinegar and a squeeze of fresh lemon juice, and blend in. Continue adding the oil slowly until it is all used up and the mixture is pale and the consistency of whipped cream. Adjust the seasoning to taste. Keep covered in the refrigerator for up to 3 days.

Red pepper mayonnaise

(for hot or cold barbecued seafood or chicken)

1 red pepper
1 quantity of mayonnaise (see previous recipe)

Place the whole pepper on the cooking grate and barbecue over Direct Medium heat. Grill until evenly charred on all sides, about 10–12 minutes, turning every 3–5 minutes. Remove the pepper from the barbecue and place in a small bag; close tightly. Leave for 10–15 minutes to steam off the skin. Take the pepper out of the bag and peel away and remove the charred skin. Cut off the top and then remove the seeds. Blend in a food processor until smooth. Remove and put aside. Clean the food processor and make the mayonnaise. Add the pepper purée to the mayonnaise and blend briefly until smooth.

Aïoli

(for barbecued vegetables, chicken or lamb)

6 plump garlic cloves, crushed
3 egg yolks
3 tablespoons fresh white breadcrumbs
4 tablespoons white wine vinegar
salt
freshly ground black pepper
300ml/^{1}/$_2$ pint extra virgin olive oil

Put the garlic, egg yolks, breadcrumbs, vinegar and plenty of seasoning in a food processor and blend to a paste. With the motor still running, slowly add the olive oil and blend to give a thick emulsified sauce. Add 1 tablespoon of boiling water and blend briefly. Keep covered in the refrigerator for up to 2 days.

Rouille

(for barbecued fish)

For a quick version of classic rouille, follow the recipe for aïoli and add 2 tablespoons of Harissa (Moroccan chilli sauce, page 21) to the egg yolks and breadcrumbs before adding the oil.

Pesto

This classic Italian dressing for pasta also makes an instant sauce to serve with sizzling hot grilled steaks, chicken or fish straight from the barbecue.

25g/1oz fresh basil leaves

150ml/¼ pint extra virgin olive oil

25g/1oz pine nuts

2 plump garlic cloves, crushed

50g/2oz Parmesan cheese, finely grated

Put the basil leaves, olive oil, pine nuts and garlic into a food processor and blend to a paste. Season well and put into a small bowl. Stir in the freshly grated Parmesan. Put into a small bowl or jar, cover with a film of olive oil and keep in the refrigerator for up to 1 week or freeze.

Fresh tomato, garlic & tarragon relish

Unlike traditional relishes, a fresh relish can be put together in no time. Vary the flavour with herbs, chillies, oils and vinegars. This one is good with most hot grilled meats, chicken or fish. Again, it tastes better if made well ahead to allow the flavours to develop.

250g/9oz baby plum tomatoes

2 plump garlic cloves, crushed

4 spring onions, finely chopped

1 tablespoon fresh tarragon, chopped

1 tablespoon balsamic vinegar

2 tablespoons extra virgin olive oil

salt

freshly ground black pepper

Cut the tomatoes in half and chop them roughly, taking care not to lose any of the tomato juices. Transfer to a mixing bowl. Stir in the crushed garlic, spring onions and tarragon. Add the vinegar and oil, season and stir well. Ideally put aside at room temperature for at least 4 hours to let the flavours develop.

Pistou

This French accompaniment is similar in name and style to its Italian cousin pesto, but does not contain cheese or pine nuts. It is particularly good with barbecued fish and vegetables, such as aubergine, peppers, courgettes and tomatoes.

4 plump garlic cloves, crushed

25g/1oz fresh basil leaves

125ml/4fl oz extra virgin olive oil

salt

freshly ground black pepper

Put the crushed garlic and basil into a food processor and process to a paste (add a splash of the oil to get it moving in the processor if you need to). Add the remaining oil and blend very well. Season well. Put into a small bowl or jar, cover with a film of olive oil and keep in the refrigerator for up to 1 week or freeze for up to 2 months.

Romesco sauce

This thick paste-like sauce takes its name from the Spanish chillies which are often used to make the sauce. It goes well with chicken, lamb, fish and grilled vegetables.

1 dried choricero or Ñora chilli, deseeded (or any other sweet mild Spanish chilli, dried)

1 red pepper

25g/1oz blanched almonds

8 tablespoons olive oil

3 garlic cloves, crushed

25g/1oz stale crustless white bread, cut into cubes

4 plum tomatoes, skinned, deseeded and chopped

2 tablespoons sherry vinegar

1 teaspoon sun-dried tomato paste

1/2 teaspoon smoked paprika

1/2 teaspoon salt

In a bowl, cover the dried chilli with hot water and soak for 20 minutes. Drain well. Put the red pepper on the cooking grate over Direct Medium heat. Grill until evenly charred on all sides, about 10–12 minutes, turning every 3–5 minutes. Remove the pepper from the heat, place in a small bag and close tightly. Leave for 10–15 minutes to steam off the skin. Remove the pepper from the bag, peel away the charred skin, cut off the top and remove the seeds. Heat a large heavy-based pan and toast the almonds until golden. Remove and put aside. Heat the oil in the pan and fry the garlic until golden. Remove with a slotted spoon and put aside. Add the bread to the pan, fry until golden and drain on kitchen paper. Keep the oil and set aside. Place all the ingredients in a food processor and blend until smooth. With the motor still running, gradually pour in the reserved oil. Keep the sauce covered in the refrigerator for one week.

Harissa (Moroccan chilli sauce)

The fiery Moroccan paste is ideal as a flavouring or an accompanying sauce. It is available in jars and tubes, but nothing beats the home-made version to add kick to any barbecued foods. This generous helping serves 8 to 10.

1 large red pepper

3 teaspoons caraway seeds

4 teaspoons cumin seeds

250g/9oz fresh medium-hot red chillies, deseeded and chopped

salt

4 plump garlic cloves, crushed

2 teaspoons sun-dried tomato paste

2 teaspoons red wine vinegar

2 teaspoons smoked paprika

6 tablespoons extra virgin olive oil

freshly ground black pepper

Put the whole pepper on the cooking grate over Direct Medium heat. Grill until evenly charred on all sides, about 10–12 minutes, turning every 3–5 minutes. Remove the pepper from the heat, place into a small bag and close tightly. Leave for 10–15 minutes to steam off the skins. Remove the pepper from the bag, peel away the charred skin. Cut off the top, remove the seeds and cut the flesh into large pieces. Put aside. Heat a small heavy-based pan on the hob and add the caraway and cumin seeds. Shake them around for a few seconds. Remove from the heat and crush roughly using a mortar and pestle. Put aside. Put the chopped chillies into a food processor with a pinch of salt, half the crushed seeds and all the garlic. Blend for 2–3 minutes until as smooth as possible. Add the pepper pieces and blend again until smooth. Transfer to a mixing bowl. Add the remaining crushed seeds, tomato paste, vinegar, paprika and olive oil. Stir well and season to taste. Put into a small bowl or jar, cover with a film of olive oil and keep in the refrigerator for up to 4 weeks or freeze.

Tzatziki (Greek yoghurt sauce)

This Greek yoghurt-based accompaniment is usually served as part of a *meze*, but is great with grilled spicy fish, chicken, lamb or vegetables. Make it well ahead, even the day before, to allow its flavours to develop.

1 cucumber
275ml/9fl oz Greek yoghurt
2 tablespoons extra virgin olive oil
4 plump garlic cloves, crushed
1 tablespoon fresh mint, chopped
salt
freshly ground black pepper

Roughly grate the cucumber. Put into a clean tea towel and squeeze out any excess juice. Put the grated cucumber into a small bowl. Add the yoghurt, oil, garlic and mint and mix well. Season to taste. If you can, leave in the refrigerator for at least 8 hours or overnight to let the flavours develop. Keep covered in the refrigerator for 3 days.

Salmoriglio

Italian cooks are famous for their variety of herb mixtures used to flavour meat. This salmoriglio mixture – an intensely flavoured no-cook herb sauce – is great with chicken or steaks fresh from the grill (page 124).

5 tablespoons fresh oregano, roughly chopped
1 teaspoon sea salt flakes
2 tablespoons lemon juice
8 tablespoons extra virgin olive oil
freshly ground black pepper

Finely grind the oregano and sea salt flakes together using a mortar and pestle. Add the lemon juice, then slowly pour in the olive oil, stirring well. Season with freshly ground black pepper. Put aside to let the flavours develop.

Easy fig & prune chutney

This thick, fruity, sweet and slightly sour-flavoured chutney works beautifully with the smoky, charred flavour of meat and game from the barbecue.

250g/9oz stoned no-need-to-soak prunes
250g/9oz dried figs
175ml/6fl oz thick runny honey
10cm/4 inch piece cinnamon stick
1 large sprig of rosemary
600ml/1 pint red wine vinegar

Roughly chop the prunes and figs. Put into a large heavy-based saucepan and add the honey, cinnamon stick, rosemary sprig and vinegar. Stir well, cover and cook over a very low heat for 35–40 minutes, stirring occasionally, leaving a bare amount of liquid. Remove from the heat and cool. Discard the cinnamon stick and rosemary twig. This chutney will keep covered in the refrigerator for up to 1 month.

Salsa verde

This no-cook Italian favourite is particularly great for adding zest to plainly cooked fish, shellfish and vegetables hot from the barbecue.

120ml/4fl oz extra virgin olive oil

6 anchovy fillets

3 tablespoons capers, drained and rinsed

1/2 lemon, juice only

1/2oz fresh parsley, roughly chopped

1/2oz fresh mint, roughly chopped

1 plump garlic clove, crushed

1 teaspoon Dijon mustard

1/2 teaspoon salt

Put all the ingredients in a food processor and blend briefly until you have a coarsely textured thick sauce. You can blend it further if you prefer it smoother. Put into a small bowl or jar, cover with a film of olive oil and keep in the refrigerator for up to 1 week or freeze for up to 2 months.

Tapenade (black olive paste)

The pungent black purée from Provence will transform any simply barbecued meat, chicken or fish. Use the best black olives you can find.

100g/4oz black olives, pitted

2 tablespoons capers in brine, drained and rinsed

2 teaspoons fresh thyme leaves

1 plump garlic clove, crushed

85ml/3fl oz extra virgin olive oil

salt

freshly ground black pepper

Put the olives, capers, thyme and garlic into a food processor and blend until smooth. With the motor still running, pour in the oil in a slow steady stream. Season well. Put into a small bowl or jar, cover with a film of olive oil and keep in the refrigerator for up to 2 weeks.

fish on the grill

Mediterranean fish & shellfish

There are hundreds of species of fish and shellfish in the Mediterranean, some that are enjoyed all over the world and others that are little more than a closely guarded local delicacy. When choosing fish for the barbecue, remember to select the freshest fish available. The fish should have a wonderful aroma of the sea and not a strong 'fishy' smell; the eyes should be bright and clear. These fish have been chosen for their versatility on the barbecue, their worldwide appeal and, most of all, their flavour.

Brill

Similar to turbot but tends to be smaller, with slightly softer-textured flesh. It can be bought on or off the bone and is ideal for the barbecue.

John Dory

Also known as St. Peter's fish – legend has it that the dark 'thumbprint' on the side of the fish is that of St. Peter's himself. It is a flat round fish that yields two large bone-free white fillets of firm flesh, with an excellent flavour, making it perfect for the barbecue.

Lobster

Lobsters are excellent when cooked on the barbecue. Once cut in half and cleaned, they are conveniently cooked in their own shells. They have firm sweet white meat in their tails and claws and are among the most satisfying seafood tastes in the world. For best results, buy live lobsters. To find out how to prepare lobsters for the barbecue, see pages 62–63.

Mackerel

An oily fish with a soft dark flesh. In the same way as sardines, mackerel are associated with sunshine and grilling outside. The most common variety weigh about 450g/1lb each, perfect for a single portion.

Monkfish

An unusually large fish that is rarely seen whole, as it's just the tail that's used, which is why some places sell it as 'monkfish tails'. Once the fish is filleted off the cartilage-like tailbone you are left with fillets of pure white fish with no bones. It has a slight sweetness to its steak-like flesh and is ideal for the barbecue as it doesn't flake when cooked. A good choice for kebabs.

Mussels & clams

These are both bivalves – shellfish that live in two hinged shells. They may not seem like the most obvious choice for the barbecue, but are in fact delicious when cooked in foil parcels with butter and a little wine. The principle is the same as cooking them in a covered pan in the kitchen. They don't really take on the flavour of the barbecue, but it's a great way to cook them for a barbecue meal. It's important to note that fresh mussels and clams should be discarded if they are dead; you will know this if they are open and won't close when lightly tapped.

Prawns

Prawns can be barbecued with their shell on or off. It is best to skewer them on long metal skewers so you can turn many of them at the same time. Buy large prawns like the Mediterranean prawn or crevette, or large black tiger prawns.

Red mullet

A coral- and orange-tinted fish. The flesh is firm and flaky, and the skin crisps when barbecued. Red mullet has a fantastic flavour, and, once gutted and scaled, is perfect for barbecuing whole. A fish of about 325g/11oz will serve one person.

Sardines

An oily fish with a soft well-flavoured dark flesh. They are rich in Omega-3 oil, which is very nutritious. They are synonymous with barbecuing all along the Mediterranean shores, and are best cooked and eaten very fresh, as the oil causes the flesh to deteriorate more rapidly.

Sea bass

A silver metallic-skinned round fish which will yield 2 thick fillets. The best-flavoured sea bass are caught wild and are often large and expensive, but more commonly available are smaller, farmed bass. An ideal fish for barbecuing with its dense soft flesh and delicate flavour. When purchased, sea bass must be gutted immediately, as they are prone to burst and this can taint the flavour of the flesh.

Sea bream

A fish that has well-flavoured and textured flesh due to its diet of crustaceans. Sea bream vary in size from about 450–900g/1–2lb, perfect for one or two people. They have a slightly oval body and big scales. The most prized is the Gilt-head bream, known as *daurade* in France.

Scallops

If you buy fresh scallops in their shells, open the shells, clean around the scallop and roe, and loosen the scallop in the bowl-shaped shell. The scallops can then be cooked on the barbecue in their shells, with little more than a squeeze of lemon juice. Scallops free of their shells are best skewered before barbecuing.

Squid

Squid comes from the family of cephalopods, from the Greek meaning 'feet coming out of heads'. Barbecuing suits squid well as it needs only to be cooked for a short time over a high heat. The flesh of squid caramelises to give it distinctive grill marks. Large squid can be cleaned, cut open and cooked flat on the cooking grate, while small squid are delicious if cleaned and stuffed before grilling (see page 67 for preparation guidelines).

Swordfish

This fish has a fantastic meaty texture that is excellent for barbecuing. It also tastes best when it is slightly undercooked. Buy it in steaks each about 325g/11oz in weight for cutting into chunks and skewering.

Tuna

Tuna is instantly recognisable by its dark red meaty loins or steaks. Like swordfish, it is tailor-made for the barbecue. The firm steaks hold together well during barbecuing and it is best undercooked, still slightly pink in the centre.

Turbot

One of the finest and most expensive fish you can buy. Turbot has thick fillets of firm white flesh, ideal for the barbecue because it remains juicy and does not tend to dry out during cooking. Fillets can be bought and barbecued on or off the bone.

Monkfish in pancetta with caper & pine-nut dressing

| main course: serves 4 | gas: direct / medium heat | charcoal: direct | prep time: 10 mins | barbecue time: 8 mins |

Pine nuts come from the giant umbrella or parasol pine cones seen looming all over the Mediterranean, especially in southern France. If pancetta is unavailable, use rindless smoked streaky bacon, but make sure it's fairly thinly sliced.

4 monkfish fillets each weighing about 175g/6oz

freshly ground black pepper

8 wafer-thin slices of pancetta

Caper and pine nut dressing

2 tablespoons pine nuts

3 tablespoons capers, drained and rinsed

4 tablespoons extra virgin olive oil

1 lemon, juice only

oil, for brushing

2 tablespoons fresh flat leaf parsley, roughly chopped

1 If using wooden or bamboo skewers, first soak 4 in cold water for 30 minutes.

2 Season the fish fillets with freshly ground black pepper. Wrap each fillet of monkfish with 2 slices of pancetta. Run a skewer through the centre of the fillet, catching the pancetta at either end to hold it in place. Put aside.

3 To make the dressing: Heat a heavy-based small pan and add the pine nuts. Toss over a high heat for 1–2 minutes, until golden and toasted all over. Remove from the pan and put aside. Add the capers to the pan with the olive oil and lemon juice, and put this aside.

4 Brush the pancetta-wrapped monkfish lightly with oil. Barbecue the fish over Direct Medium heat for 6–8 minutes, turning once.

5 Meanwhile, put the pan of dressing on the heat and warm it gently over a low heat. Season with freshly ground black pepper and stir in the pine nuts.

6 Remove the skewers from the fish and arrange the fish on a platter. Spoon over the warm dressing and scatter with the chopped parsley.

DID YOU KNOW? A favourite in healthful Mediterranean diets, pine nuts are small, pellet-shaped and creamy white in colour with a sweet, rich flavour and high in oil. They are also known as *piñon* in Spain, and *pignola* in Italy where the variety is richer.

Whole red mullet in anchovy, olive & plum tomato sauce

| **main course:** serves 4 | **gas:** direct / medium heat | **charcoal:** direct | **prep time:** 25 mins | **barbecue time:** 8 mins |

Plum tomatoes are common all over the Mediterranean and have an excellent flavour for cooking. They vary a lot in size; for this sauce you need five large plum tomatoes but, if small, use about nine or ten.

Anchovy, olive & plum tomato sauce

2 tablespoons olive oil

3 plump garlic cloves, crushed

20 small black olives

4 anchovy fillets in olive oil, drained and coarsely chopped

3 tablespoons sun-dried tomato purée

5 plum tomatoes, skinned, deseeded and chopped

good pinch of sugar

salt

freshly ground black pepper

3 tablespoons fresh parsley, chopped

8 whole red mullet, each weighing about 175–200g/6–7oz, scaled, gutted and fins trimmed

oil, for brushing

1 To make the sauce: Heat the olive oil in a saucepan and cook the garlic for 2–3 minutes until soft. Add the olives and anchovies, and cook for 2–3 minutes, stirring occasionally until the anchovies dissolve to a pulp. Add the tomato purée, chopped tomatoes and sugar, and cook for 5 minutes. Season and stir in the chopped parsley. Put aside.

2 Brush the fish with oil and season well. Barbecue over Direct Medium heat for 6–8 minutes, turning once until cooked through.

3 Put the fish on a serving platter, spoon over the hot sauce and serve immediately.

Red mullet wrapped in vine leaves

main course: serves 4	gas: direct / medium heat	charcoal: direct	prep time: 10 mins	barbecue time: 8 mins

The vine leaves in this easy Moroccan-inspired dish are perfect for keeping the red mullet moist as it cooks. They will also help to impart a delicate flavour to make this dish even more delicious.

8 vine leaves, fresh or preserved in brine

4 red mullet, each weighing about 200g/7oz, scaled and gutted

olive oil, for brushing

salt

freshly ground black pepper

lemon wedges, to serve

1 If using fresh vine leaves, drop them into a pan of boiling water for a few seconds until they just flop and loose their stiffness. If using leaves in brine, soak them briefly in hot water to remove the salt. Next, drain and wash the fresh or pre-prepared leaves under cold running water, then pat dry. Cut out the tough stem of each leaf.

2 Wash the fish inside and out, and pat dry with kitchen paper. Lay 2 vine leaves on a work surface, shiny side down and slightly overlapping. Brush with a little olive oil, place a fish across the leaves and season well. Fold the leaves around the fish so that the head just sticks out. Put aside and repeat with the remaining leaves and fish.

3 Brush the fish parcels with a little oil, and barbecue over Direct Medium heat for 6–8 minutes, turning once. Serve with wedges of lemon.

DID YOU KNOW? Fresh vine leaves are great if you can find them but you can also use leaves preserved in brine which may be easier to find, or you can make them yourself. To preserve vine leaves you must wash the leaves and leave them to dry first. Tie small amounts into a bundle and fix with thread. Fold the leaves into a thick roll and arrange them in a tall glass container with a lid. Pour over hot water mixed with salt until the container is almost filled. Leave to cool and then close the container tightly and store it in the refrigerator for about a month.

Whole mackerel with fresh coriander & chilli dressing

| main course: serves 4 | gas: direct / medium heat | charcoal: direct | prep time: 5 mins | barbecue time: 10 mins |

This is a great quick dish from Morocco designed to make the most of the freshness of just-caught fish. The ingredients in the dressing are left raw, but very finely chopped to help their flavour penetrate the cooked mackerel.

Fresh coriander and chilli dressing

2 shallots, very finely chopped

2 plump garlic cloves, crushed

1 fresh red chilli, deseeded and chopped

6 tablespoons extra virgin olive oil

1 lemon, juice only

4 tablespoons fresh coriander, chopped

4 mackerel each weighing about 350g/12oz, gutted

oil, for brushing

salt

freshly ground black pepper

couscous, to serve

1 To make the dressing: Put the shallots, garlic, chilli, olive oil, lemon juice and coriander into a small bowl and mix well. Put aside until ready to use, to let the flavours develop.

2 Make 3–4 deep slashes on each side of each mackerel. Brush the mackerel with a little oil and season inside and out. Barbecue over Direct Medium heat for 8–10 minutes, turning once halfway through the cooking time.

3 Put the cooked fish on a warm platter, pour over the dressing and leave for about 5 minutes to let the flavours infuse the fish. Serve with couscous.

Sardines with green olive, orange & parsley dressing

appetiser: serves 4	gas: direct / medium heat	charcoal: direct	prep time: 30 mins + marinating	barbecue time: 6 mins

In Spain, sardines are usually grilled over charcoal or wood fires, which produces the most memorable taste. The flavours of the olives, orange zest and parsley works brilliantly with the oiliness of the fish.

675g/1½lb sardines, scaled and heads removed

½ tablespoon sea salt

Olive, orange and parsley dressing

5 tablespoons fresh parsley, roughly chopped

2 plump garlic cloves, crushed

1 small orange, grated zest only

50g/2oz plump green stoned olives, chopped

oil, for brushing

freshly ground black pepper

lemon wedges, to serve

1 Cut each fish open down to the tail and remove the gut. **1** Open the fish out like a book. **2** Place belly-side down on a board. Press firmly along the backbone until the fish is completely flat. **3** Turn the fish over and pull away the backbone, snipping it off at the tail end with scissors. Remove any small bones left behind in the fillet. Repeat with all the sardines. Wash the sardines inside and out under cold running water. Pat dry with kitchen paper and put onto a large tray. Sprinkle over the sea salt. Cover and chill for about 30 minutes.

2 Meanwhile, to make the dressing: Put the parsley, garlic, orange zest and olives into a bowl and mix well. Cover and chill until required.

3 Brush the sardines with oil and season with pepper. Barbecue over Direct Medium heat for 2–6 minutes, turning once, until tender. (For sardines measuring 5–10cm/2–4 inches in size, cook for 2–4 minutes, turning once. For sardines up to 10–20cm/8 inches long, cook for about 4–6 minutes, turning once.)

4 Arrange the sardines on a platter and scatter with the olive, orange and parsley dressing. Serve with wedges of lemon.

Sardines with tomato, parsley & garlic stuffing

main course: serves 4	gas: direct / medium heat	charcoal: direct	prep time: 30 mins	barbecue time: 6 mins

Sardines are a staple of the Mediterranean diet. Removing the bones makes the sardines more pleasant to eat, but if you find this task a bit fiddly, ask your fishmonger to do it for you. Salting the filleted sardines adds flavour and helps to firm up the flesh before they are barbecued.

675g/1½lb fresh sardines, scaled and heads removed

½ tablespoon sea salt

Tomato, parsley and garlic stuffing

8 tablespoons fresh parsley, chopped

4 plump garlic cloves, crushed

4 tablespoons plain dried breadcrumbs

3 plum tomatoes, finely chopped

salt

freshly ground black pepper

1 lemon, juice only

oil, for brushing and drizzling

1 Cut each fish down to the tail and remove the guts. Open the fish out like a book and place, belly-side down, on the board. Press firmly along the backbone until the fish is completely flat. Turn the fish over and pull away the backbone, snipping it off at the tail end with scissors. Remove any small bones left behind in the fillet. Repeat with all the sardines (see pages 34–35). Wash the sardines inside and out under cold running water. Pat dry with kitchen paper and put on to a large tray. Sprinkle over the sea salt. Cover and chill for about 30 minutes.

2 To make the stuffing: Put 6 tablespoons of the parsley into a bowl, with the garlic, breadcrumbs and tomatoes, and plenty of seasoning. Mix well and put aside.

3 Squeeze the lemon juice over the fish and season. Put a large spoonful of the stuffing down the centre of each fish and close each one up again. Secure with a cocktail stick. Brush the sardines with oil and season.

4 Barbecue the sardines over Direct Medium heat for 2–6 minutes, turning once, until tender. (For sardines measuring 5–10cm/ 2–4 inches in size, cook for 2–4 minutes, turning once. For sardines up to 20cm/8 inches long, cook for about 4–6 minutes, turning once.)

5 Arrange the cooked sardines on a platter, drizzle with a little extra virgin olive oil and scatter with the remaining parsley.

Fish steaks with hot tomato & caper dressing

main course: serves 4	gas: direct / medium heat	charcoal: direct	prep time: 5 mins	barbecue time: 8 mins

Tuna and swordfish can be cut into thick steaks for barbecuing, since these hold together very well. They should only be cooked until slightly pink in the centre, to prevent them from drying out. The addition of harissa to the sauce is typically Moroccan, and adds that essential colour and 'bite' to the fish steaks.

Hot tomato and caper dressing

2 tablespoons capers, drained

6 tablespoons extra virgin olive oil

1 lemon, juice only

2 tomatoes, deseeded and diced

1 teaspoon Harissa (page 21)

2 tablespoons fresh coriander, chopped

salt

freshly ground black pepper

4 tuna or swordfish steaks, each weighing about 175g/6oz

oil, for brushing

boiled new potatoes, to serve

1 To make the dressing: Soak the capers in cold water for a few minutes to remove excess vinegar or brine. Drain and put into a saucepan with the olive oil, lemon juice, tomatoes, harissa and coriander. Season and stir well. Put aside.

2 Brush the fish steaks with oil and season. Barbecue over Direct Medium heat for 6–8 minutes, turning once. This should give you a steak that is opaque in the centre.

3 Meanwhile, heat the dressing in the saucepan, without allowing it to boil. Put the fish steaks on 4 plates and spoon over the dressing. Serve with boiled new potatoes dressed with butter and chopped mint.

DID YOU KNOW? The caper shrub can be found in semi-arid climes and grows wild and abundantly around many areas of the Mediterranean. The pink and white flowers of the caper shrub bloom for just one day. It is the buds of the un-opened flowers that become the condiment we call capers.

Cheese-stuffed swordfish rolls with lemon butter

| main course: serves 4 | gas: direct / medium heat | charcoal: direct | prep time: 30 mins | barbecue time: 10 mins |

In Italy, cheese is a staple of the kitchen and is used to flavour many traditional recipes. Since fish cooks quickly, it's important to grate and cut the cheese very small, so it melts into the stuffing in the time it takes the fish rolls to cook through. If Provolone cheese is unavailable, use all Parmesan instead.

Stuffing

75g/3oz crustless stale bread

1 tablespoon olive oil

25g/1oz Parmesan cheese, roughly grated

50g/2oz Provolone cheese, cut into small dice

1 tablespoon capers, drained, rinsed and roughly chopped

2 tablespoons fresh parsley, chopped

15g/$\frac{1}{2}$oz butter, chilled

salt

freshly ground black pepper

675–900g/1$\frac{1}{2}$–2lb lean swordfish or 8 x 100g/4oz thin slices of swordfish

oil, for brushing

Lemon butter

1 lemon, juice only

100g/4oz butter, chilled

1 tablespoon fresh parsley, chopped

1 If using wooden or bamboo skewers, soak 4 in cold water for at least 30 minutes.

2 To make the stuffing: Crumble the bread into a large bowl. Add the oil and 1 tablespoon water. Mix together with your hands to soften the bread. Add the Parmesan, Provolone, capers and chopped parsley. Cut the firm chilled butter into small dice and add to the bowl. Season lightly as the cheese is salty. With your hands, squeeze together to form a soft dough.

3 Cut the swordfish into 8 slices about 5mm/$\frac{1}{4}$ inch thick. Place the swordfish slices on a clean work surface. **1** Divide the stuffing into 8 and put in the centre of each fish slice. **2** Roll up the fish. Secure each by threading 2 rolls on to a skewer.

4 Brush the swordfish rolls with a little oil and season with salt and pepper. **3** Barbecue over Direct Medium heat for 8–10 minutes, turning once.

5 Meanwhile, to make the lemon butter: Heat the lemon juice in a small pan. Cut the chilled butter into small dice and whisk into the lemon juice a little at a time. Stir in the parsley and season well. Serve with the swordfish rolls.

Swordfish or tuna steaks with fennel & chilli dressing

| **main course:** serves 6 | **gas:** direct / medium heat | **charcoal:** direct | **prep time:** 25 mins + marinating | **barbecue time:** 10 mins |

Fennel grows wild all over the Mediterranean. It belongs to the same family as dill, having similar feathery leaves, but has a much more pronounced aniseed flavour. In this dish the fish steaks are rubbed with the mixture before barbecuing.

Fennel and chilli dressing

6 red chillies, deseeded and finely chopped

4 tablespoons fresh leaf fennel, chopped

150ml/¼ pint extra virgin olive oil

2 lemons, juice only

salt

freshly ground black pepper

1 tablespoon dried fennel seeds

3 plump garlic cloves, crushed

¼ teaspoon dried chilli flakes

6 tuna or swordfish steaks each weighing about 225g/8oz

100ml/3½fl oz extra virgin olive oil

1 lemon, juice only

1 To make the sauce: Put the chillies, chopped fennel herb, olive oil and the lemon juice into a bowl with plenty of seasoning and whisk well. Put aside.

2 Heat a small heavy-based pan on the hob. Add the fennel seeds and shake them around for a few seconds until their aroma rises. Remove from the heat and crush the fennel seeds finely using a mortar and pestle. Transfer to a small bowl and add the garlic and dried chilli flakes. Season and mix well.

3 Lay the fish steaks on a clean work surface and rub half of the fennel, garlic and chilli mixture over each steak. Turn the steaks over and rub in the remaining mixture. Put the fish steaks into a large shallow flat dish in a single layer. Mix the olive oil with the lemon juice and pour over the fish. Cover and leave in the refrigerator for 30 minutes to marinate.

4 Remove the fish steaks from the marinade and discard the leftover marinade. Barbecue the fish steaks over Direct Medium heat for 8–10 minutes, turning once. This should give you a steak cooked, but slightly pink in the middle. Serve with the fennel and chilli dressing.

Swordfish kebabs with bay leaves

main course: serves 4	gas: direct / medium heat	charcoal: direct	prep time: 15 mins + marinating	barbecue time: 8 mins

Popular in Spain, fresh swordfish is commonly used for these simple kebabs as the flesh won't flake easily and will hold it's shape, but you can use any firm-fleshed fish that will hold well on a skewer.

4 swordfish steaks, each weighing 200–225g/7–8oz

16 fresh bay leaves

1 onion, roughly chopped

6 tablespoons olive oil

½ lemon, juice only

salt

freshly ground black pepper

Orange and watercress salad (page 183), to serve

1 If using wooden or bamboo skewers, soak 4 in cold water for at least 30 minutes.

2 Cut the swordfish steaks into 2.5cm/1 inch cubes. Thread these on the skewers, alternating with the bay leaves. Put into a shallow dish.

3 Put the onion into a food processor, together with the olive oil, lemon juice and seasoning. Blend to an almost smooth pulp. Pour over the kebabs, cover and leave to marinate in the refrigerator for at least 30 minutes.

4 Season the kebabs with salt and pepper, and barbecue over Direct Medium heat for 6–8 minutes, turning once and brushing again with any remaining marinade. Serve with the orange and watercress salad.

DID YOU KNOW? Bay leaves come from the sweet bay or laurel tree, known as Laurus nobili, and can be used in soups, stews, meat and vegetable dishes. The leaves also flavour classic French dishes such as bouillabaise and bouillon.

Tuna niçoise barbecue style

main course: serves 8	gas: direct / medium heat	charcoal: direct	prep time: 45 mins	barbecue time: 8 mins

The world-famous Provençal salad is given the barbecue treatment, grilling fresh tuna steaks over hot coals and serving them warm on the classic salad of broad beans, green beans, tomatoes, cucumber, boiled eggs, olives and anchovies.

Niçoise dressing

1 shallot, very finely chopped

2 plump garlic cloves, crushed

8 tablespoons extra virgin olive oil

3 tablespoons white wine vinegar

salt

freshly ground black pepper

225g/8oz baby spinach leaves

350g/12oz broad beans, shelled and blanched

350g/12oz fine green beans, trimmed and blanched

1 small cucumber, diced

250g/9oz cherry tomatoes, halved

6 eggs, just hard-boiled

6 tuna steaks, each weighing 175–200g/6–7oz

oil, for brushing

12 anchovy fillets, drained

24 black olives

large handful of fresh basil leaves

fresh crusty bread, to serve

1 To make the niçoise dressing: Put the shallot, garlic, olive oil, vinegar and seasoning into a small bowl and whisk well. Put aside to let the flavours develop.

2 Put the spinach leaves, broad beans, green beans, cucumber and tomatoes into a large shallow bowl and toss well together. Pile onto a large platter and put aside. Shell the hard-boiled eggs, cut them into halves or quarters and put aside.

3 Brush the tuna steaks with oil and season well. Barbecue over Direct Medium heat for 6–8 minutes, turning once. This should give you a steak that is cooked but slightly pink in the middle. Remove and put straight onto the salad on the platter.

4 Put the egg halves around the edge of the salad and scatter with the anchovy fillets and olives. Whisk the dressing again, drizzle over the salad steaks and scatter with basil leaves. Serve with lots of fresh crusty bread.

Fish cakes with aïoli

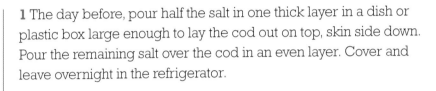

| main course: serves 4 | gas: direct / medium heat | charcoal: direct | prep time: 40 mins + salting overnight | barbecue time: 10 mins |

Brandade is a traditional French dish combining poached salt cod with olive oil, milk and garlic, to give a soft purée. Here the flavour is used to make fish cakes, with the added taste of the barbecue. Salting your own cod gives a much fresher flavour than ready-salted. If you choose to use ready-salted cod, such as *bacalao* from Spain, you will need to soak it in cold water for at least 48 hours, changing the water regularly.

100g/4oz table salt

550g/1¼lb thick unskinned cod fillet

600ml/1 pint milk

500g/1lb 2oz floury potatoes

2 tablespoons olive oil

3 plump garlic cloves, crushed

freshly ground black pepper

1 tablespoon fresh parsley, chopped

1 tablespoon fresh chives, chopped

50g/2oz plain flour, for dusting

Aïoli (page 19), to serve

1 The day before, pour half the salt in one thick layer in a dish or plastic box large enough to lay the cod out on top, skin side down. Pour the remaining salt over the cod in an even layer. Cover and leave overnight in the refrigerator.

2 The next day, rinse the cod, cover with fresh cold water and leave to soak for 1 hour.

3 Drain the fish and put into a saucepan with the milk. Bring to the boil and cook for 6–8 minutes until just tender. Remove from the heat and drain off the milk. Once the cooked fish is cool enough to handle, remove the skin and any bones and flake into big pieces.

4 Meanwhile, cut the potatoes into evenly sized pieces and cook in boiling salted water for 20 minutes until tender. Drain well and return the saucepan to the heat for about 1 minute, shaking the pan over the heat to dry off any excess moisture.

5 Add the olive oil to the potatoes with the crushed garlic and plenty of black pepper and mash until smooth. Add the parsley, chives and flaked fish, and fold through the potatoes until well combined. Divide the mixture into 8 and shape each into a fish cake. Put on a tray and chill for at least 30 minutes to firm up.

6 Dust each fish cake all over with flour, shaking off any excess. Barbecue over Direct Medium heat for 8–10 minutes, turning once, until well marked by the grill. Serve with fresh aïoli.

Fish fillets with roasted peppers & tomatoes

| main course: serves 4 | gas: direct / medium heat | charcoal: direct | prep time: 20 mins + marinating | barbecue time: 20 mins |

This dish takes its inspiration from traditional French *pipérade*, a mixture of tomatoes and peppers stewed in olive oil, and is cooked in a pan with scrambled eggs. For this barbecued version, however, the peppers, onions and tomatoes are first barbecued, then flavoured with fresh herbs and served with grilled marinated fish.

4 fish fillets, such as turbot, brill, John Dory, sea bass, sea bream, sole or monkfish, each weighing about 225g/8oz

2 tablespoons fresh thyme, chopped

1 tablespoon fresh rosemary, chopped

9 tablespoons olive oil

salt

freshly ground black pepper

1 red onion

1 red pepper

1 green pepper

4 large plum tomatoes

2 tablespoons fresh parsley, chopped

1 Put the fish fillets into a shallow dish large enough to hold them in one layer. Mix 1 tablespoon of the thyme and the rosemary with 3 tablespoons of the olive oil. Season well and pour over the fish. Leave to marinate in the refrigerator for 30 minutes.

2 Meanwhile, cut the onion into slices about 1.5cm/½ inch thick. Cut the top and bottom off the peppers, then cut the pepper into rings about 1.5cm/½ inch thick, shaking out the seeds as you go. Halve the plum tomatoes. Put all the vegetables into a large bowl and toss with 2 tablespoons of the olive oil and some salt and pepper.

3 Arrange the vegetables on the cooking grate with the cut side of the tomatoes facing up. Barbecue over Direct Medium heat for 8–10 minutes, turning once. Transfer to a bowl and sprinkle with the remaining 4 tablespoons of olive oil, the remaining 1 tablespoon of thyme and the chopped parsley and toss well.

4 Remove the fish from the herby marinade and discard any leftover marinade. Barbecue the fish fillets over Direct Medium heat for 5–10 minutes, according to the thickness, turning once.

5 Put the vegetables on a large platter and top with the hot fish.

Sea bass fillets with fresh herbs & lemon

| main course: serves 6 | gas: direct / medium heat | charcoal: direct | prep time: 15 mins | barbecue time: 7 mins |

This typical Italian dish uses both fresh herbs and lemons on the fish during grilling as well as in a tangy sauce to pour over the cooked fish. Sea bass, turbot and brill all vary greatly in size, so your fillets may range in thickness. Try to use pieces of fish which are about 2.5–4cm/1–1½ inches thick, so you can make deep slashes to embed the herbs.

6 thick fillets of sea bass, turbot or brill, each weighing 175–200g/6–7oz

2 tablespoons fresh marjoram, roughly chopped

2 tablespoons fresh basil, roughly chopped

2 tablespoons fresh mint, roughly chopped

2 tablespoons fresh dill, roughly chopped

salt

freshly ground black pepper

oil, for brushing

4 lemons

100ml/3½fl oz extra virgin olive oil

1 Rinse the fillets and pat dry on kitchen paper. Make 3 or 4 deep slashes in the skin side of the fish, making sure not to cut all the way through.

2 Mix all the herbs together and push as much of the herb mixture as you can into each slash. You will have some herbs left over which you will use later. Season the fillets well on both sides and brush lightly with oil. Cut all the lemons in half.

3 Barbecue the fillets, flesh side down first, together with 6 lemon halves, cut side down, over Direct Medium heat for 5–7 minutes, turning the fish once until just tender.

4 Meanwhile, squeeze the juice of the remaining 2 lemon halves into a bowl, whisk in the olive oil and season well.

5 Arrange the fish on a platter surrounded by the seared lemon halves and pour over the lemon dressing. Scatter with the remaining herbs.

DID YOU KNOW? If a recipe calls for both lemon juice and zest it is always best to pour the juice over the zest to keep it moist and flavourful.

Fish fillets
with stifado sauce

| main course: serves 4 | gas: direct / medium heat | charcoal: direct | prep time: 1 hour | barbecue time: 10 mins |

Stifado is traditionally a casserole-baked Greek stew of meat, poultry or fish, with tomatoes, baby onions, white wine, garlic and herbs. For this version, a stifado sauce is made to serve with barbecued fish fillets of your choice.

8 tablespoons olive oil

3 bay leaves

3 cloves

freshly ground black pepper

2 garlic cloves, crushed

900g/2lb baby white onions or shallots, peeled

120ml/4fl oz red wine

2 x 400g/14oz cans of chopped tomatoes

1 tablespoon fresh parsley, finely chopped

3 tablespoons fresh leaf fennel, finely chopped

50ml/2fl oz white wine vinegar

salt

900g/2lb firm fish fillets, such as red mullet, turbot, brill, John Dory or sea bass or a mixture

oil, for brushing

1 Put 5 tablespoons of olive oil into a large saucepan and heat until hot but not smoking. Add the bay leaves, cloves and a few twists of black pepper, and sizzle for 2–3 minutes. Add the garlic and onions or shallots, and stir well. Cover, reduce the heat and cook very gently for 20 minutes, stirring occasionally.

2 Add the red wine and the chopped tomatoes, cover and cook gently for 15–20 minutes, until the onions are tender. Uncover and simmer for a further 15–20 minutes, until thickened and the onions are very soft. Stir in the remaining 3 tablespoons of oil, the chopped herbs, vinegar and 1 teaspoon of salt.

3 Brush the fish fillets with oil and season. Barbecue the fish over Direct Medium heat for 5–10 minutes according to thickness, turning once. Arrange in a large shallow serving dish. Spoon the sauce over and around the fish and serve.

Whole fish with sweet moroccan lemon sauce

main course: serves 4	gas: indirect / medium heat	charcoal: indirect	prep time: 45–55 mins	barbecue time: 15 mins

In the Moroccan kitchen, sweet and tangy flavours are used together in sauces, marinades, and ingredients. Be guided by your fishmonger or local fisherman as to the best and freshest catch of the day to use in your recipe.

4 tablespoons olive oil

450g/1lb onions, sliced

2 tablespoons raisins

2 tablespoons runny honey

1 lemon, juice and zest

salt

freshly ground black pepper

4 whole fish, such as sea bass, red snapper, sea bream, trout, sole or John Dory, each weighing about 350–450g/12oz–1lb, scaled, gutted and fins trimmed

oil, for brushing

fresh parsley, chopped, to garnish

1 Heat the oil in a saucepan, add the sliced onions, cover and cook over a very low heat for 30–35 minutes, stirring occasionally, until very soft. Uncover, increase the heat, add the raisins and cook for a further 4–5 minutes, until lightly golden.

2 Add the honey, lemon juice and zest, and seasoning. Cook for a further 5 minutes. Remove from the heat and put aside.

3 Wash the fish inside and out and pat dry with kitchen paper. Brush the fish with oil and season well. Barbecue the fish over Indirect Medium heat for 10–15 minutes, turning once.

4 Arrange the fish on a platter or 4 plates and top with the warm lemon, honey and raisin-flavoured onions. Garnish with chopped fresh parsley.

Pissaladière

| appetiser or light lunch: serves 6 | gas: direct / medium heat | charcoal: direct | prep time: 45 mins + resting | barbecue time: 8 mins |

This delicious open tart from southern France bears more than a passing resemblance to Italian pizza. It makes a great accompaniment to pre-dinner drinks. Look for a good-quality brand of canned anchovies, preferably French or Italian.

2 teaspoons easy-blend dried yeast

1 teaspoon sugar

350g/12oz plain flour

1 teaspoon salt

1½ tablespoons olive oil

Topping

6 tablespoons olive oil

4 large red onions, thinly sliced

3 plump garlic cloves, crushed

200g/7oz can of chopped tomatoes

1 tablespoon sun-dried tomato paste

2 tablespoons fresh oregano, chopped

2 teaspoons caster sugar

salt

freshly ground black pepper

oil, for brushing

100g/4oz anchovy fillets in olive oil, drained

32 black olives

1 In a large bowl, mix the yeast, sugar, flour and salt. Make a well in the centre and add 200ml/7fl oz of warm water and the olive oil. Mix well to make a dough. Knead the dough lightly on a floured surface until smooth. Put into a clean, large bowl, cover and leave to rise in a warm place until doubled in size.

2 Meanwhile, make the topping: Heat the oil in a large saucepan, add the onions and garlic and cook over a low heat for 15–20 minutes until very soft, stirring occasionally. Add the tomatoes, tomato paste and oregano, and simmer gently for 5 minutes. Remove the lid, add the sugar, season well and cook for a further 2–3 minutes, until thickened and reduced slightly.

3 Knead the dough for a few minutes. Divide it into 2 pieces and roll each to a round base about 25.5cm/10 inches in diameter. Brush one side of each base with oil. Slide the bases onto 2 baking trays.

4 Slide the bases, oiled side down, onto the cooking grate and cook over Direct Medium heat for 2–3 minutes, until the grill marks are visible. Slide back onto the baking sheet and turn over so the grilled side is facing up.

5 Divide the onion mixture between each base and spread evenly with the back of a spoon. Cut the anchovy fillets in two lengthwise. Arranged the anchovy fillets on top in a criss-cross pattern. Put a black olive between each cross.

6 Slide the pissaladières back on to the cooking grate and cook for 4–5 minutes, until the edges of the crust are golden. Cut into thin wedges and serve warm.

Marinara pizza

main course: serves 4	gas: direct / medium heat	charcoal: direct	prep time: 30 mins + resting	barbecue time: 9 mins

Pizza is, of course, Italian in origin. Here, the ingredients are adapted for this simple pizza that requires minimal cooking, the secret being to use very ripe plum tomatoes, good quality buffalo mozzarella and a good brand of canned Italian tuna.

2 teaspoons easy-blend dried yeast

1 teaspoon sugar

350g/12oz plain flour

1 teaspoon salt

1½ tablespoons olive oil

Topping

6 ripe plum tomatoes

18 black olives

2 tablespoons extra virgin olive oil, plus more for brushing

salt

freshly ground black pepper

200g/7oz can of good-quality Italian tuna in olive oil, drained

12 large cooked prawns, peeled and heads removed

225g/8oz buffalo mozzarella, or 2 mozzarella cheeses, drained

large handful of wild rocket leaves

splash of balsamic vinegar

1 In a large bowl, mix the yeast, sugar, flour and salt. Make a well in the centre and add 200ml/7fl oz of warm water and olive oil. Mix well to make a dough. Knead the dough lightly on a floured surface until smooth. Put into a clean large bowl, cover and leave to rise in a warm place until doubled in size.

2 Meanwhile, to make the topping: Halve and deseed the tomatoes, then cut the flesh into small dice. Put into a small bowl with the olives and a splash of olive oil. Season and put aside.

3 Knead the dough once more for a few minutes. Divide it in 2 and roll each piece into a pizza base about 25.5cm/10 inches in diameter. Brush one side of each pizza base with olive oil. Slide the bases on to 2 large baking trays.

4 Slide the bases, oiled side down, onto the cooking grate and cook over Direct Medium heat for 2–3 minutes, until the grill marks are visible. Slide back on to the baking sheet and turn over so the grilled side is facing up.

5 Divide the tomato and olive mixture between each base. Arrange the tuna and prawns over the tomato and olive mixture. Tear the mozzarella into small pieces and scatter on top.

6 Slide the pizzas back on to the cooking grate and cook for 5–6 minutes, until the prawns are cooked and the cheese has melted. Remove from the heat and top each with a handful of rocket leaves. Drizzle the leaves with a splash of olive oil and a splash of balsamic vinegar. Serve half a pizza per person.

Scallop & prosciutto spiedini with fresh rosemary

| main course: serves 6 | gas: direct / medium heat | charcoal: direct | prep time: 20 mins + marinating | barbecue time: 6 mins |

Spiedini in Italy means 'skewered' or 'spitted' and can apply to meat or fish dishes. Here the skewers are made from rosemary branches. These branches need to come from a fairly mature bush, so they are strong enough to skewer the ingredients without bending or breaking. Otherwise use soaked wooden skewers.

6 fresh rosemary branches, each about 15cm/6 inches long

24 large fresh scallops

6 tablespoons olive oil

1 lemon, juice only

salt

freshly ground black pepper

1 red onion

12 slices of prosciutto

Salsa verde, to serve (page 23)

1 Pull most of the leaves off the rosemary branches, leaving just a tuft of rosemary. Roughly chop half the rosemary leaves at the tip (you won't need all of it).

2 Put the scallops (and orange roe, if using) into a large bowl. Sprinkle over 1 tablespoon of the chopped rosemary. Add the olive oil, lemon juice and season to taste. Toss well and leave in the refrigerator for 30 minutes to marinate.

3 Cut the red onion into 6 wedges and dismantle each wedge into layers. Cut each slice of prosciutto into 2 wide strips.

4 Take a scallop and shake off the excess marinade. Wrap a strip of prosciutto around the scallop, overlapping the ends. Secure the prosciutto in place by skewering with a rosemary branch. Next, thread on a layer of onion wedge. Continue until all the scallops, prosciutto, onion and rosemary stalks are used, to give 6 *spiedini* in all.

5 Brush the *spiedini* with a little of the rosemary marinade and then discard any leftover marinade. Barbecue the *spiedini* over Direct Medium heat for 4–6 minutes, turning once, until just tender. Serve with salsa verde.

DID YOU KNOW? If you are lucky, your fishmonger will sell scallops still in their shell with their bright orange roe still attached – the roe is completely edible and as delicious as the actual scallop.

Mussels in saffron butter with chorizo

| appetiser: serves 4 | gas: indirect / medium heat | charcoal: indirect | prep time: 25 mins | barbecue time: 12 mins |

The mussels don't really take on the flavour of the barbecue as they are sealed in parcels, but this is a really easy and efficient way to cook them and makes a complementary starter to a barbecue dinner party.

1.75 kg/4–4½lb mussels

large pinch of saffron strands

1 plump garlic clove, crushed

1 shallot, very finely chopped

100g/4oz chorizo (cured Spanish sausage)

2 tablespoons fresh parsley, chopped

175g/6oz butter, softened

4 tablespoons white wine

freshly ground black pepper

1 Wash and scrub the mussels under cold running water and remove the tough fibrous beard protruding from between the firmly closed shells. Discard any shells that are open and refuse to shut when lightly tapped with a knife. Put the cleaned mussels aside.

2 Crush the saffron strands to a fine powder using a mortar and pestle. Transfer to a large bowl and add the garlic and shallot (it's very important that the shallot is very finely chopped). Cut the chorizo into thin slices, then into very small dice and add to the bowl. Stir in the chopped parsley. Add the softened butter and beat all the ingredients together. Add the wine a tablespoon at a time, beating well between each addition. Season well with pepper.

3 Take 2 large sheets of heavy-duty foil and lay one on top of the other. Put a quarter of the mussels in the middle. Dot the mussels with a quarter of the saffron and chorizo butter. Bring the sides of the foil up around the mussels to form a bowl shape, then bring the edges of the foil together and seal to make a loose parcel. Repeat with more foil and the remaining mussels and butter to make 4 parcels in all.

4 Barbecue over Indirect Medium heat for 10–12 minutes until all the mussels have opened. Let your guests open their own parcel and enjoy the fresh aroma that's released. Any mussels that have refused to open should be discarded.

Clams cooked in chilli cream sauce

main course: serves 4	gas: indirect / medium heat	charcoal: direct	prep time: 25 mins	barbecue time: 12 mins

There are many varieties and sizes of clams, but it is best to look for small ones, about 2.5–5cm/1–2 inches in size. These are known as *vongole* in Italy and in this variation the clams are steamed in their own juices together with some chilli, before being combined with the pasta.

2 tablespoons olive oil

4 garlic cloves, crushed

3 red chillies, deseeded and finely chopped

4 tablespoons fresh parsley, chopped

200ml/7fl oz crème fraîche

salt

freshly ground black pepper

1.5kg/3–3½lb small clams

350g/12oz linguini or spaghettini

2 lemons, to serve

1 Heat the oil in a small pan and cook the garlic and chilli gently over a low heat for 6–8 minutes, stirring occasionally, until softened. Remove from the heat, transfer to a bowl and leave to cool.

2 When completely cold, stir in the chopped parsley and the crème fraîche, and season well. Wash the clams and discard any shells that are open and refuse to shut when lightly tapped with a knife.

3 Take 2 large sheets of heavy-duty foil and lay one on top of the other. Put a quarter of the clams in the middle. Add a quarter of the chilli cream. Bring the sides of the foil up around the clams to form a bowl shape, then bring the edges of the foil together and seal to give a loose parcel. Repeat with more foil and the remaining clams and chilli cream to make 4 parcels in all.

4 Barbecue over Indirect Medium heat for 10–12 minutes, until all the clams have opened. Discard any clams that have not opened.

5 Meanwhile, cook the linguini according to the packet instructions or until al dente. Drain well and toss with a little olive oil.

6 Open the clam parcels and spill into 4 large pasta bowls. Top each with linguini and serve with a lemon half.

Lobster spanish style

| **main course:** serves 6 | **gas:** direct / medium heat | **charcoal:** direct | **prep time:** 35 mins | **barbecue time:** 15 mins |

The full-flavoured Catalan sauce for this recipe is a classic from Spain, made in a similar way to French aïoli but without eggs. It can be made up to a day in advance and is great with most grilled shellfish.

Catalan sauce

175ml/6fl oz olive oil

50ml/2fl oz dry sherry

2 tablespoons red wine vinegar

1 ripe plum tomato, skinned

3 plump garlic cloves, crushed

4 tablespoons ground almonds

large pinch of dried red chilli flakes

salt

freshly ground black pepper

2 tablespoons fresh parsley, chopped

3 live lobsters each weighing about 675g/1½lb

25g/1oz butter, melted, for brushing

lemon wedges, to serve

1 To make the Catalan sauce: Put the olive oil, sherry and vinegar into a bowl, whisk together well and put aside.

2 Roughly cut up the skinned tomato and put into a food processor with the garlic, almonds, chilli flakes and a little seasoning. Blend until puréed. With the motor still running, slowly drizzle in the oil and sherry mixture to give a smooth thick sauce. Stir in the chopped parsley. Put aside.

3 To prepare the lobsters, put them in the freezer for 1 hour. Then remove them and lay each on a chopping board with the head pointing towards you. Insert the tip of a sharp chopping knife where the tail meets the head and swiftly split the head in two. Repeat with the tail so the lobster is now split in two lengthwise. Remove the stomach sac (a small, clear pouch found in the head section) and the greenish livers. Also lift out the intestinal tract from the tail section. Crack the shell of the lobster claws with the back of the knife (see pages 62–63).

4 Brush the cut sides of the lobsters with melted butter and season lightly. Place them on the cooking grate, shell side down, and barbecue over Direct Medium heat for 10–15 minutes until tender.

5 Transfer to a platter and serve with the sauce and a lemon wedge on the side.

Lobster greek style

| main course: serves 4 | gas: direct / medium heat | charcoal: direct | prep time: 50 mins | barbecue time: 15 mins |

Barbecuing is an easy way to cook lobsters. Traditionally, Greek fisherman first split the live lobsters in half, but if you find this a little daunting, pop the lobsters into the freezer for about 1 hour. This painless method makes them very sluggish and easier to work with. Alternatively, quickly dip them into boiling water before splitting them.

3 tablespoons olive oil

2 shallots, chopped

3 plump garlic cloves, crushed

1 small fennel bulb, finely chopped

pinch of saffron strands

150ml/¼ pint medium sweet white wine

6 plum tomatoes, skinned and chopped

2 bay leaves

3 tablespoons fresh mint, roughly chopped

½ small lemon, juice only

salt

freshly ground black pepper

2 live lobsters, each weighing about 675g/1½lb

saffron-flavoured rice, to serve

1 Heat the oil in a large saucepan, add the shallots and garlic and cook for 4–5 minutes, until softened but without colour. Add the chopped fennel, cover and cook for 5–6 minutes.

2 Grind the saffron to a powder using a mortar and pestle. Add to the pan with the wine and cook, uncovered, over a high heat until the liquid is reduced to a few tablespoons. Add the tomatoes and bay leaves and cook for 15–20 minutes until very thick and pulpy.

3 Stir in 2 tablespoons of the mint and squeeze in the lemon juice. Season well and put aside.

4 To prepare the lobsters, put them in the freezer for 1 hour. Then remove them and lay each on the chopping board with the head pointing towards you. **1** Insert the tip of a sharp chopping knife where the tail meets the head and swiftly split the head in two. **2** Repeat with the tail so the lobster is now split in two lengthwise. Remove the stomach sac (a small, clear pouch found in the head section) and the greenish livers. **3** Also lift out the intestinal tract from the tail section. Crack the shell of the lobster claws with the back of the knife. Lightly season the meat of the lobster and then spoon the thick tomato and fennel mixture over the tail meat in each lobster half.

5 Place the lobsters on the cooking grate, shell side down, and barbecue over Direct Medium heat for 10–15 minutes until tender.

6 Scatter the remaining chopped mint over the lobster. Serve with a mild saffron-flavoured rice.

Prawns with tomato sauce & feta cheese

main course: serves 4 appetiser: serves 6	gas: direct / medium heat	charcoal: direct	prep time: 1 hour	barbecue time: 6 mins

This dish combines two key flavours that are the mainstay of Greek cuisine, feta cheese and ouzo. The saltiness of the cheese complements the spirit's fresh aniseed flavour and by using the freshest prawns available, you will also achieve the best texture.

2 tablespoons olive oil

1 small onion, finely chopped

2 plump garlic cloves, crushed

675g/1½lb plum tomatoes, skinned and roughly chopped

1 large bay leaf

1 cinnamon stick

900g/2lb large raw prawns, heads removed only

oil, for spraying or brushing

175g/6oz feta cheese, crumbled

freshly ground black pepper

ouzo, to taste (optional)

fresh crusty bread, to serve

1 Heat the olive oil in a large saucepan. Add the onion and garlic, and cook for 4–5 minutes, until softened but without colour. Add the chopped tomatoes, bay leaf and cinnamon stick. Bring to the boil, reduce the heat and cook very gently for 35–40 minutes, until thickened. Keep hot.

2 Meanwhile, thread the prawns in their shells onto long skewers. It doesn't matter how many skewers you use, as you won't be serving them on the skewers. (Remember, if using wooden or bamboo skewers, make sure you have soaked them first in cold water for at least 30 minutes to prevent them from scorching.)

3 Lightly spray or brush the prawns with oil, and barbecue over Direct Medium heat for 4–6 minutes, turning once, until cooked through.

4 Meanwhile, stir half the feta into the hot sauce. Remove the cinnamon stick, then pour the sauce into a large shallow serving dish. Use a fork to push the prawns off the skewers directly into the tomato sauce. Scatter with the remaining feta cheese and season with freshly ground black pepper (you won't need salt as the prawns and feta will be salty enough).

5 If using the ouzo, splash about a tablespoon over the prawns and feta. Serve with plenty of fresh crusty bread.

Calamari with lemon & thyme dressing

| appetiser: serves 4 | gas: direct / high heat | charcoal: direct | prep time: 15 mins | barbecue time: 4 mins |

All around the Greek islands, small cafés on the docks grill and serve calamari fresh off the boat, as part of a *meze* of a variety of fish, salads and olives. Quick grilling over a high heat is the secret to perfectly cooked calamari that isn't rubbery.

4 medium-sized calamari (about 675g/1¹/₂lb total weight)

Lemon and thyme dressing

1 lemon, juice only

2 teaspoons Dijon mustard

3 tablespoons extra virgin olive oil

1 heaped tablespoon fresh thyme, finely chopped

freshly ground black pepper

oil, for brushing

rocket leaves, to serve

1 First prepare the calamari: **1** Pull the head and tentacles from the body. The intestines will come away with the tentacles. Reach into the body and pull out any remaining intestines with the plastic-like quill. **2** Pull the purple skin off the body. Pull off the two fins and remove the purple skin from these too. Wash out the body, then cut down one side to open out flat. **3** Cut the tentacles from the head; from just in front of the eyes, in one piece. Squeeze out the beak-like mouth from the centre of the tentacles. Once you have discarded all the innards you should have the opened-out body, two fins and the tentacles.

2 Using a serrated knife, score the inner side of the body with parallel lines spaced about 1cm/¹/₂ inch apart. **4** Then score in the opposite direction to give a crisscross pattern, making sure you don't cut all the way through.

3 To make the dressing: Put the lemon juice and mustard in a small bowl and whisk together. Slowly drizzle in the oil and continue whisking until you have a cloudy dressing. Stir in the thyme and season with the pepper.

4 Brush the calamari with oil and season with pepper only. Barbecue, scored side down, over Direct High heat for 1–2 minutes, turn over and cook for a further 1–2 minutes, until just curled up. Remove the calamari from the grill and arrange on a large serving platter and drizzle over the dressing. Serve with rocket leaves.

poultry on the grill

Whole roast chicken
with chorizo

main course: serves 4	**gas:** indirect / medium heat	**charcoal:** indirect	**prep time:** 15 mins	**barbecue time:** 1–1¼ hours

This is a delicious adaptation of a classic oven-roasted dish from the Balearic Islands of Spain in which the warm spicy oils from the chorizo sausage trickles into the chicken breast as it slowly barbecues.

1.5kg/3–3½lb free-range chicken

100g/4oz chorizo, thinly sliced

1 large Spanish onion, halved

few large sprigs of fresh thyme

3 tablespoons olive oil

½ teaspoon ground cinnamon

salt

freshly ground black pepper

grilled peppers, crisp green salad and fresh crusty bread, to serve

1 Carefully, work your fingers between the skin and the breast meat of the chicken. As you ease your fingers further under the skin, it will become loose, ready for stuffing. Continue in the same manner to loosen the meat on the legs.

2 If the chorizo is not already sliced, cut into thin slices. Work the slices up under the loosened skin, until all the slices are used up and all of the breast and most of the leg meat are covered.

3 Stuff the bird's cavity with the onion halves and the sprigs of thyme. Tie the legs together with string and tuck the wing tips underneath the bird to give it a neat shape. Mix the olive oil and cinnamon together and season very well. Use to brush all over the chicken, reserving the remainder to brush the chicken again during cooking.

4 Season the chicken with salt and pepper and barbecue over Indirect Medium heat for 1–1¼ hours, brushing once more halfway through the cooking time, until the juices run clear when a knife is inserted in to the thickest part of the thigh.

5 Leave the chicken to rest for 10 minutes before carving. Serve with grilled peppers, a crisp green salad and fresh crusty bread.

Paprika chicken with chickpeas

| main course: serves 4 | gas: indirect / medium heat | charcoal: indirect | prep time: 40 mins | barbecue time: 1 hour |

Whole barbecued chicken, flavoured with smoked paprika and served with a traditional thick Spanish stew of chickpeas, chorizo, new potatoes and hot chilli.

1.5kg/3–3¹⁄₂lb free-range chicken

2 tablespoons olive oil

1–2 teaspoon(s) Spanish smoked paprika

salt

freshly ground black pepper

Spanish stew

675g/1¹⁄₂lb baby new potatoes, halved

3 tablespoons olive oil

1 onion, chopped

225g/8oz piece of chorizo, skinned and cut into small dice

1 teaspoon dried chilli flakes

4 garlic cloves, crushed

450g/1lb vine-ripened tomatoes, skinned and roughly chopped

400g/14oz can of chickpeas, drained and rinsed

2 bay leaves

4 tablespoons fresh parsley, chopped

1 Spatchcock the chicken: **1** Using poultry shears or large kitchen scissors, cut along either side of the backbone of the chicken and remove. **2** Open the bird out flat and put, skin-side up, on a board, and using the palm of your hand, press down hard on the breastbone to flatten. **3** Push a skewer through one wing to come out diagonally through the leg on the other side. Criss-cross with another skewer through the other leg and wing.

2 Mix the olive oil with the paprika into a smooth paste. Brush the chicken all over with paprika oil and season. Barbecue the chicken over Indirect Medium heat for 50 minutes to 1 hour, brushing once more with the paprika oil halfway through cooking, until the juices run clear when the thickest part of the thigh is pierced with a knife.

3 To make the stew: Cover the potatoes with cold salted water, and bring to the boil. Reduce the heat and simmer for 10–15 minutes, until just tender. Drain well and set aside.

4 Heat the olive oil in a large frying pan and cook the onion for 3–4 minutes until softened. Add the chorizo and cook for 4–5 minutes until lightly golden. Remove the chorizo and set aside. Add the chilli flakes and garlic to the pan, and cook for 1 minute. Add the tomatoes, chickpeas and bay leaves, and stir-fry for 1–2 minutes. Return the chorizo to the pan with 150ml/¹⁄₄ pint water. Simmer for 8–10 minutes, stirring occasionally. Add the potatoes to the pan. Simmer 3–4 minutes until heated through. Remove from the heat.

5 Remove the cooked chicken to a chopping board and leave to stand for 10 minutes. Stir 3 tablespoons of the chopped parsley into the stew and spoon onto a platter. Cut the chicken into quarters and place on top of the stew. Sprinkle with the remaining parsley.

Chicken devil style

main course: serves 6–8	gas: indirect / medium heat	charcoal: indirect	prep time: 20 mins + marinating	barbecue time: 1 hour

Chicken devil style, or *pollo alla diavola*, to give it its proper Italian name, is so named because of its fiery ingredients, dried chilli flakes and black peppercorns. Chillies are dried naturally in the sun in many Mediterranean countries as this increases the flavour and can also help to speed up the drying process. Feel free to decrease or increase the amount of chilli flakes and peppercorns according to your taste.

2 x 1.5kg/3–3^{1}/$_{2}$lb oven-ready chickens

1 tablespoon black peppercorns

1 tablespoon dried chilli flakes

3 lemons, juice only

175ml/6fl oz extra virgin olive oil

salt

herb salad, to serve

1 Spatchcock the chickens (see pages 72–73).

2 Put the chickens into a large shallow dish. Roughly crush the black peppercorns using a mortar and pestle. Add the dried chilli flakes and crush a little more, but not too finely. Put aside. Mix the juice of 2 of the lemons with 120ml/4fl oz of the olive oil. Pour over the chickens, then sprinkle over about three-quarters of the pepper and chilli mixture. Cover with cling film and marinate in the refrigerator for at least 1 hour.

3 Mix the remaining lemon juice, olive oil, pepper and chilli mixture together. Remove the chickens from the marinade and discard any remaining marinade from the dish. Season with salt. Barbecue the chickens over Indirect Medium heat for 50 minutes to 1 hour, brushing with the peppercorn mixture every 20 minutes, until the juices run clear when the thickest part of the thigh is pierced with a knife. Remove from the barbecue and leave to stand for 10 minutes before cutting up.

4 Divide each chicken into quarters and serve with a delicious herb salad.

Whole chicken stuffed with sweet garlic & tarragon

main course: serves 6–8	gas: indirect / medium heat	charcoal: indirect	prep time: 30 mins	barbecue time: 2¼ hours

The garlic in this recipe is roasted on the barbecue first, which takes away its pungent raw flavour and leaves you with a mild sweet garlic paste, perfect when combined with fresh tarragon in this southern French dish.

3 heads of garlic

3 teaspoons olive oil

75g/3oz butter, softened

75g/3oz full-fat soft cream cheese

1 lemon

2 shallots, very finely chopped

75g/3oz button mushrooms, very finely chopped

2 tablespoons fresh parsley, chopped

2 tablespoons fresh tarragon, chopped

1.75–2.25kg/4–5 lb oven-ready chicken

salt

freshly ground black pepper

1 Remove the loose white papery skin from the heads of garlic, leaving the cloves exposed but still intact. Cut across the head to cut off the tips of the cloves. Drizzle each cut head with a teaspoon of olive oil. Wrap each head loosely in foil and barbecue over Indirect Medium heat for 45 minutes, until very tender. Remove and put aside to cool.

2 Unwrap and squeeze the soft garlic from each clove into a bowl. Add the soft butter, cream cheese and the juice of the lemon, and beat well until smooth. Stir in the shallots, mushrooms, parsley and tarragon. Season, stir well and put aside. Reserve the squeezed-out lemon.

3 Carefully, work your fingers between the skin and the breast meat of the chicken. As you ease your fingers further under the skin, it will become loose, ready for stuffing. Continue loosening the meat on the legs. Work all the garlic and butter mixture up under the loosened skin, until all the breast and most of the leg meat is covered. Put the squeezed-out lemon into the cavity.

4 Season the chicken with salt and pepper and barbecue over Indirect Medium heat for 1¼–1½ hours, until the juices run clear when a knife is inserted to the thickest part of the thigh. Leave to rest for 10 minutes before carving.

Ginger-marinated chicken
with sweet tomato jam

| **main course:** serves 4 | **gas:** indirect / medium heat | **charcoal:** indirect | **prep time:** 30 mins + marinating | **barbecue time:** 1 hour |

Honey and cinnamon provide the sweet and spicy flavours in this thick, pulpy tomato jam from Morocco, which is served hot with this simple, fragrant barbecued chicken.

Marinade

large pinch of saffron strands

2 garlic cloves, crushed

$^1/_4$ teaspoon ground ginger

$^1/_2$ teaspoon freshly ground black pepper

4 tablespoons olive oil

1.5kg/3–3$^1/_2$lb free-range chicken

Sweet tomato jam

2 tablespoons olive oil

1 onion, finely chopped

900g/2lb ripe plum tomatoes, skinned and chopped

2 tablespoons sun-dried tomato paste

1 teaspoon ground cinnamon

3 tablespoons thick dark honey

2 tablespoons fresh coriander, chopped

salt

freshly ground black pepper

1 To make the marinade: Crush the saffron finely, using a mortar and pestle and put into a small bowl. Add the crushed garlic, ginger, pepper and oil, and mix well. Put aside.

2 Spatchcock the chicken (see pages 72–73).

3 Rub the saffron and ginger mixture all over the skin side of the chicken. Cover with cling film and marinate in the refrigerator for at least 4 hours.

4 Barbecue the chicken over Indirect Medium heat for 50 minutes to 1 hour, until the juices run clear when the thickest part of the thigh is pierced with a knife.

5 While the chicken is cooking, make the sweet tomato jam. Heat the oil in a saucepan and cook the onion for 3–4 minutes, until softened. Add the tomatoes and tomato paste, cover and cook over a gentle heat for 15 minutes. Uncover and cook for a further 15–20 minutes, until very much softened and thickened. Add the cinnamon and honey, and cook for a further 10 minutes, stirring occasionally. Stir in the coriander and season well.

6 Remove the cooked chicken from the barbecue and leave to rest for 10 minutes. Cut into 4 portions and serve with the sweet tomato jam.

Chicken tapas

| appetiser: serves 4–6 | gas: direct / medium heat | charcoal: direct | prep time: 15 mins + marinating | barbecue time: 10 mins |

This is a very popular tapas from the Andalucia region of Spain, made with Moorish spices that marinate chunks of chicken or lean pork fillet. It is traditionally served with a bowl of pickled chillies and sherry.

large pinch of saffron strands

1/2 teaspoon coriander seeds

1/2 teaspoon cumin seeds

1/2 teaspoon fennel seeds

1 teaspoon sweet paprika

2 plump garlic cloves, crushed

2–3 tablespoons fresh oregano, roughly chopped

1 fresh bay leaf, finely chopped

2 teaspoons red wine vinegar

2 teaspoons olive oil

salt

freshly ground black pepper

450g/1lb lean, boneless skinless chicken

pickled chillies, to serve

1 Soak the saffron in a tablespoon of boiling salted water for 10 minutes.

2 Put the coriander, cumin and fennel seeds into a small frying pan and dry-fry for a few seconds, shaking the pan from side to side until their aroma rises. Crush using a mortar and pestle and transfer to a large bowl.

3 Into the ground seeds, stir in the saffron with its water, paprika, crushed garlic, oregano, bay leaf and vinegar. Stir in the oil, season and mix well. Cut the chicken into 2.5cm/1 inch cubes, add to the mixture and stir well. Cover and leave to marinate in the refrigerator for 2 hours. Soak 8 short wooden or bamboo skewers in cold water for at least 30 minutes.

4 Thread the chicken onto the soaked skewers and season with salt and pepper. Barbecue the chicken skewers over Direct Medium heat for 8–10 minutes, turning once. Serve with pickled chillies and glasses of chilled sherry, if desired.

DID YOU KNOW? Saffron held the esteemed position of being considered a 'luxury' spice in the Middle Ages. It was rare and expensive, produced in only three places: Albi and the Languedoc, Aquila in Abruzzi, and in Catalonia. It was used in the preparation of medications and to dye cloth, but mostly as a flavouring – it is integral to Mediterranean dishes such as bouillabaise, risotto Milanese, and paella.

Chicken & artichoke skewers

| main course: serves 4 | gas: direct / medium heat | charcoal: direct | prep time: 25 mins | barbecue time: 10 mins |

For these skewers you can use any cut of skinless, boneless chicken you like, such as thighs – which often have more flavour than breast meat. Also, use a dark, thick, Greek-style honey, rather than the more runny English honeys, if you can.

675g/1½lb lean boneless, skinless chicken

large bunch of spring onions

400g/14oz can of artichoke hearts

3 lemons

2 teaspoons fresh thyme, chopped

3 tablespoons thick Greek-style honey

3 tablespoons olive oil

salt

freshly ground black pepper

200g/7oz Greek yoghurt

1–2 tablespoon(s) Tapenade (page 23)

Greek salad (page 182), to serve

1 If using wooden or bamboo skewers, soak 8 in cold water for at least 30 minutes.

2 Cut the chicken into 2.5cm/1 inch pieces. Cut the spring onions into short lengths. Drain the artichokes and rinse under cold running water, then pat dry on kitchen paper. Cut each artichoke in half. Cut 2 of the lemons into quarters, then cut each quarter into 2 wedges. Thread the chicken, spring onion pieces, artichoke hearts and lemon wedges alternating on the 8 skewers. Put aside.

3 Squeeze the juice from the remaining lemon and put into a bowl. Add the thyme, honey and olive oil, and whisk well to amalgamate the honey and oil. Season and whisk again. Use to brush all over the skewers.

4 Barbecue the skewers over Direct Medium heat for 8–10 minutes, turning once and brushing (use a clean basting brush) with the remaining marinade.

5 Meanwhile, mix the Greek yoghurt and the tapenade together. Serve with the kebabs, and accompany with a Greek salad.

Chicken & green olive skewers

| **main course:** serves 4 | **gas:** direct / medium heat | **charcoal:** direct | **prep time:** 20 mins + marinating | **barbecue time:** 10 mins |

To give a really authentic flavour to this dish, look for good plump Spanish olives, such as Seville manzanilla green olives, which are widely exported. They are big, sweet and meaty, with a fine texture. You could also use stuffed green olives.

Marinade

1 tablespoon olive oil

2 tablespoons brandy

85ml/3fl oz dry sherry

1/2 plump garlic clove, crushed

1/2 teaspoon fresh thyme, chopped

1/4 teaspoon fennel seeds, crushed

salt

freshly ground black pepper

450g/1lb chicken breast fillets or boneless, skinless chicken breasts, cut into strips

1 red onion

16 plump green Spanish olives, pitted

Spanish rice salad (page 185), to serve

1 To make the marinade: Mix the olive oil, brandy, sherry, garlic, thyme, fennel seeds and plenty of seasoning in a mixing bowl. Put the chicken into a large shallow dish and pour the marinade over it. Cover and leave to marinate in the refrigerator for 2 hours. If using wooden or bamboo skewers, soak 4 of them in cold water for at least 30 minutes.

2 Cut the red onion into wedges and separate the layers. Put aside. Drain the chicken and reserve the marinade.

3 Thread a few onion layers on to a skewer, then thread 3 chicken strips and 4 olives onto the skewer and finish with a few more onion pieces (see picture on page 68). Make 4 skewers in all. Brush all over with the marinade and season lightly. Discard the leftover marinade.

4 Barbecue the chicken skewers over Direct Medium heat for 8–10 minutes, turning once. Serve with a Spanish rice salad.

DID YOU KNOW? All olives will change to a black colour if left to ripen on the tree. Green olives are young fruit picked at the first stage of maturity before they begin to ripen. The size of a green olive is determined by the type of tree from which it comes, not by how early it is picked. The young olives go through a curing process to achieve the bright and snappy flavour for which they are esteemed.

Saffron & orange chicken with smoky pepper sauce

| **main course:** serves 4 | **gas:** direct / medium heat | **charcoal:** direct | **prep time:** 30 mins + marinating | **barbecue time:** 27 mins |

Here the warm colours and flavours of saffron and orange together with the smoky flavours of chargrilled peppers and Serrano ham will immediately transport you to the coast of southern Spain.

large pinch of saffron strands

2 oranges, grated zest only

2 teaspoons fresh thyme, chopped

8 tablespoons olive oil

salt

freshly ground black pepper

4 boneless chicken breasts, with skin on

4 red peppers

oil, for brushing

1 small onion, finely chopped

2 plump garlic cloves, crushed

100g/4oz Serrano ham, chopped

400g/14oz can of chopped plum tomatoes

2 tablespoons fresh parsley, chopped

1 Soak the saffron in 1 tablespoon of boiling salted water for 10 minutes.

2 Put the orange zest, thyme, saffron with its water, 6 tablespoons of the oil and plenty of seasoning into a bowl and mix very well. Put the chicken breasts into a large shallow dish and pour the marinade over it. Brush the marinade well into the chicken. Cover and leave in the refrigerator for at least 4 hours, turning occasionally.

3 About an hour before you want to cook the chicken, brush the peppers with oil. Barbecue them over Direct Medium heat until they are evenly charred on all sides, for about 10–12 minutes, turning every 3–5 minutes. Remove from the heat, place in a bag and close tightly. Leave for 10–15 minutes to steam off the skins. Once cool enough to handle, remove the peppers from the bag and peel away the charred skins. Cut off the tops and remove the seeds, then chop the flesh finely.

4 Heat the remaining 2 tablespoons of olive oil in a saucepan and cook the onion and garlic for 3–4 minutes until softened. Add the chopped ham and cook for a further 2–3 minutes. Add the peppers and tomatoes, cover and cook for 15 minutes until thickened. Stir in the chopped parsley and some seasoning to taste.

5 Remove the chicken from the dish and discard any marinade. Season the chicken with salt and pepper and barbecue over Direct Medium heat for 10–12 minutes, turning once. Check the seasoning in the sauce, adjust if necessary and serve with the chicken breasts.

Charred basil chicken with porcini risotto

| main course: serves 4 | gas: direct / medium heat | charcoal: direct | prep time: 35 mins + marinating | barbecue time: 12 mins |

Italy is famous for its mushroom risotto, and porcini mushrooms are very popular and easy to find. A reliable kitchen timer is a must here, as you need to cook the risotto and chicken so that both are ready at roughly the same time. Risottos don't like to hang around once they are cooked and the chicken is best eaten hot from the barbecue.

Marinade

50g/2oz fresh basil leaves

85ml/3fl oz olive oil

1 tablespoon white wine vinegar

salt

freshly ground black pepper

4 boneless, skinless chicken breasts

Porcini risotto

25g/1oz porcini mushrooms

750ml/1¼ pints hot chicken stock

2 small shallots, chopped

40g/1½oz Parmesan cheese, finely grated

50g/2oz butter

200g/7oz risotto rice

50ml/2fl oz dry white wine

1 To make the marinade: Put the basil leaves, olive oil, vinegar and some seasoning into a food processor and blend to a purée.

2 Make 5 or 6 deep slashes in the chicken breasts. Put the chicken breasts, slashed side up, into a large shallow dish, pour the basil marinade over it and use a brush to rub the marinade into the slashes. Cover with cling film and leave to marinate in the refrigerator for at least 4 hours.

3 To make the risotto: Soak the porcini mushrooms in 300ml/½ pint of boiling water for 30 minutes. Meanwhile, prepare all the ingredients for the risotto: heat the stock, chop the shallots and grate the cheese.

4 When the marinating time is up, make the risotto. Strain the liquid off the mushrooms into the stock. Chop the mushrooms and put aside. Bring the stock to the boil, then reduce to a bare simmer. Melt 25g/1oz of the butter in a large frying pan and add the chopped shallot. Cook for 3–4 minutes, until the shallot is softened. Add the mushrooms and rice and cook over the heat for about 1 minute until all the rice looks translucent. Add the wine and cook over a high heat until almost reduced to nothing. Next, add a ladleful of the hot stock, which should bubble the second it hits the pan. Continue to simmer, stirring continuously, until all that stock is almost absorbed. Then add another ladleful of hot stock and simmer and stir until absorbed again. Continue in this way until all the stock is used up and you have a tender thick, wet mixture. This will take about 20 minutes.

5 Halfway through the cooking of the risotto, remove the chicken from the marinade and discard any leftover marinade. Cook the chicken, by barbecuing over Direct Medium heat for 10–12 minutes, turning once.

6 Stir the remaining butter and the Parmesan into the risotto until just melted through. Check the seasoning (you may or may not have to add salt, depending on how salty your stock and Parmesan are).

7 Divide the risotto between 4 large plates and top with the barbecued chicken. It's important to serve the risotto straight away, otherwise the rice will continue to absorb the moisture and the risotto will become dense and overcooked.

Chicken fillets with tahini, aubergines & goat cheese

appetiser: serves 6	gas: direct / medium heat	charcoal: direct	prep time: 15 mins + marinating	barbecue time: 11 mins

This is a wonderful Greek *meze* to serve as an appetiser or at lunch. It borrows tahini, a sesame seed paste, from its Middle Eastern neighbours, to marinate and flavour the chicken, as does the sweet mint to flavour the aubergines.

1/4 teaspoon ground cumin

1/2 lemon, juice only

3 tablespoons tahini

9 tablespoons olive oil

salt

freshly ground black pepper

450g/1lb chicken fillets or boneless, skinless chicken breasts, cut into thick strips

3 garlic cloves, crushed

2 tablespoons white wine vinegar

2 teaspoons sugar

2 aubergines, cut into 1.5cm/ 1/2 inch slices

olive oil, for brushing

handful of fresh mint, chopped

350g/12oz creamy goat cheese

warm pitta bread, to serve

1 Put the ground cumin, 2 tablespoons of lemon juice, the tahini and 6 tablespoons of olive oil into a large bowl and whisk well. Season and add the chicken fillets or strips of chicken breast. Cover with cling film, put in the refrigerator and leave to marinate for 2 hours.

2 To make the dressing for the aubergines, put the remaining 3 tablespoons of olive oil into a small pan and heat gently. Add the garlic and cook over a very gentle heat for 1–2 minutes, until softened but not browned. Add the white wine vinegar and sugar, and cook for 30 seconds to 1 minute. Remove from the heat and put aside.

3 Brush both sides of the aubergine slices with plenty of oil and season well. Lift the chicken strips out of the marinade and season with salt. Discard any leftover marinade. Barbecue the chicken strips for 5 minutes on each side over Direct Medium heat, placing the aubergine slices alongside and cooking these for 6 minutes, turning once, until tender.

4 Remove the chicken from the barbecue and put into a warm serving dish. Put the aubergine slices into another serving dish. Stir the chopped mint into the cooled aubergine dressing and season well. Spoon the dressing over the aubergines. Serve with the soft goat cheese and plenty of warm pitta bread.

DID YOU KNOW? Goat cheese comes in a multitude of shapes from cones to logs and pyramids. They can sometimes be wrapped in grape leaves and rubbed with ash as an added flavour enhancer.

Chicken rissoles & treviso sauce

main course: serves 4	gas: direct / medium heat	charcoal: direct	prep time: 40 mins + chilling	barbecue time: 10 mins

Some dishes in Italy are borrowed from the Jewish communities that have been there for hundreds of years. These delicious rissoles, here adapted for the barbecue, are among them. The sauce comes from the town of the same name in northern Italy.

550g/1¼lb minced chicken (or boneless, skinless chicken breasts, minced)

1 egg, beaten

50g/2oz fresh white breadcrumbs

2 tablespoons fresh tarragon, chopped

good pinch of ground cinnamon

salt

freshly ground black pepper

flour, for dusting

Treviso sauce

4 tablespoons extra virgin olive oil

1 shallot, finely chopped

1 small carrot, very finely diced

100g/4oz prosciutto, finely chopped

3 anchovy fillets in olive oil, drained and chopped

1 lemon, grated zest only

300g/10oz chicken livers, cleaned and finely chopped

5 tablespoons dry white wine

1 tablespoon white wine vinegar

1 teaspoon ground black pepper

175ml/6fl oz chicken stock

2 tablespoons fresh parsley, chopped

1 Put the minced chicken into a large bowl. Add the egg, bread-crumbs, tarragon, cinnamon and plenty of seasoning, and mix well. Divide the mixture into 12. Using lightly floured hands, shape each into a rissole about the size of a large, slightly flattened meatball. Put on a plate and chill for at least 30 minutes to firm them up.

2 To make the sauce: Heat the olive oil in a medium-sized saucepan and add the shallot, carrot and prosciutto, and cook for 3–4 minutes, until the onion has softened. Add the anchovies, 1 teaspoon of the lemon zest and the chicken livers, and cook for 5 minutes, stirring continuously. Add the wine, wine vinegar and pepper, and cook for 5 minutes. Add the chicken stock and cook for a further 10 minutes, until reduced slightly and thickened. Stir in the chopped parsley and check the seasoning for salt, if necessary (remember, anchovies are quite salty). Put aside.

3 Brush the rissoles with oil, and barbecue over Direct Medium heat for 8–10 minutes, turning once and brushing again with oil, until cooked through. Serve with the warm Treviso sauce.

Rosemary chicken on a butter bean & feta salad

| main course: serves 4 | gas: indirect / medium heat | charcoal: indirect | prep time: 25 mins + marinating | barbecue time: 40 mins |

Rosemary and lemon are the signature flavours for Greek-style grilled chicken, here served with a chunky bean and feta salad with black olives and cos lettuce.

Rosemary marinade

150ml/¼ pint olive oil

1 lemon, juice and pared rind

2 tablespoons fresh rosemary, roughly chopped

sea salt

freshly ground black pepper

4 medium-sized chicken legs, cut into thighs and drumsticks

Butter bean and feta salad

4 tablespoons olive oil

1 shallot, very finely chopped

2 plump garlic cloves, crushed

100g/4oz kalamata black olives

2 x 400g/14oz cans of butter beans, drained and rinsed

2 tablespoons fresh parsley, chopped

½ lemon, juice only

350g/12oz feta cheese

1 or 2 cos lettuces

1 To make the marinade: Put the oil, lemon juice and rind, rosemary and seasoning into a medium-sized bowl and mix together very well. Arrange the chicken thighs and drumsticks in a single layer in a large shallow dish and pour the marinade over them. Cover with cling film and marinate in the refrigerator for 1 hour.

2 To make the salad: Heat the olive oil in a large pan and cook the shallot and garlic over a low heat for 8–10 minutes, until very soft. Add the olives, butter beans, parsley and lemon juice, and warm through for about 1 minute. Season well, remove from the heat and leave to cool completely.

3 Remove the chicken from the dish and reserve the marinade. Pour the marinade into a small saucepan, bring to the boil for 1 full minute. Remove from the heat and set aside. Season the chicken pieces with salt and pepper and barbecue over Indirect Medium heat for 35–40 minutes, turning and brushing with a little more of the reserved marinade once halfway through the cooking time.

4 Roughly crumble the feta and toss with the butter bean salad. Break the cos lettuce into leaves and arrange on a platter. Spoon over the butter bean and feta salad. Top with the grilled rosemary chicken and serve.

Chicken legs stuffed with spinach & almonds

| main course: serves 4 | gas: indirect / medium heat | charcoal: indirect | prep time: 40 mins + chilling | barbecue time: 35 mins |

Charmoula is a classic hot aromatic spice mixture from North Africa and works beautifully with the creamy spinach stuffing in the barbecued chicken.

1 egg yolk

3 tablespoons double cream

25g/1oz ground almonds

75g/3oz baby spinach

salt

freshly ground black pepper

4 chicken legs

Charmoula butter

175g/6oz butter, softened

2 tablespoons fresh coriander, chopped

2 plump garlic cloves, crushed

1½ teaspoons ground cumin

1½ teaspoons paprika

½ red chilli, deseeded and chopped

large pinch of saffron strands, crushed to a fine powder

1 lemon, grated zest only

oil, for brushing

rocket salad, to serve

1 Put the egg yolk, cream and almonds into a small bowl and beat well. Put aside.

2 Put the spinach leaves into a small pan with just the water that clings to them after washing. Cover and cook for 1–2 minutes until just wilted. Drain and then squeeze as dry as possible. Chop finely and stir into the almond mixture. Season very well.

3 Remove the thigh bones from the chicken legs: **1** Using a sharp knife, find the end of the thigh bone and scrape back the meat until the whole bone is exposed. Cut at the joint and remove the bone completely. **2** Divide the stuffing into 4 and use to fill the cavity in each leg where the thigh bone was. **3** Fold the skin around the stuffing and secure each with 2 cocktail sticks (if using wooden cocktail sticks, soak in cold water for 30 minutes first). Put aside.

4 To make the charmoula butter: Put the softened butter into a large bowl with the coriander, garlic, cumin, paprika, chilli, saffron, lemon zest and seasoning. Beat with a wooden spoon until well combined. Spoon the butter onto a large sheet of greaseproof paper or foil. Roll up the butter neatly inside the paper or foil into a log shape, then secure the ends like a Christmas cracker. Chill in the refrigerator to firm up.

5 Brush the chicken legs with oil and season with salt and pepper. Barbecue over Indirect Medium heat for 30–35 minutes, turning once.

6 Cut the butter into thick slices and serve on top of the hot chicken. Serve with a rocket salad.

Provençal duck breasts with puréed lentils

| main course: serves 4 | gas: direct / low heat | charcoal: direct | prep time: 35 mins + marinating | barbecue time: 12 mins |

Puy lentils are native to France and are by far the most superior of the lentil family. These tiny grey-green lentils hold their shape well, have a wonderful earthy flavour and are often served with roast duck. These versatile pulses make good bedfellows with woody herbs like the thyme and rosemary in this dish. Due to their high fat content, check the duck breasts on the barbecue every few minutes for the first 5 or 6 minutes, to make sure they are not flaring up.

4 duck breasts

1 teaspoon fresh thyme, chopped

1 teaspoon fresh rosemary, chopped

2 garlic cloves, crushed

1 teaspoon sea salt

1/2 teaspoon black peppercorns, roughly crushed

Lentil purée

350g/12oz Puy lentils, washed

1 onion, halved

1 carrot, cut into 3 pieces

2 bay leaves

sprig of fresh thyme

2 plump garlic cloves

1.2 litres/2 pints good chicken stock

75g/3oz unsalted butter

2 shallots, finely chopped

salt

freshly ground black pepper

sprigs of fresh rosemary, to garnish

1 Using a sharp knife, cut off any excess fat or skin that overhangs the edge of the duck breasts. The skin has a very high fat content, which is why it's important to trim off the excess to avoid flare-ups. Score the fat in a diamond pattern, cutting the fat right through to the flesh. Be sure you don't cut into the meat. Put aside.

2 In a small bowl, mix the chopped thyme and rosemary, garlic, sea salt and crushed black peppercorns. Use to rub into both sides of the duck breasts. Cover and marinate in the refrigerator for at least 2 hours.

3 To make the lentil purée: Put the lentils into a saucepan with the onion, carrot, bay leaves, thyme sprig, garlic and chicken stock. Bring to the boil, reduce the heat and simmer for 15–20 minutes, until tender. Drain the lentils, reserving the cooking liquid and discard the onion, carrot, bay, thyme and garlic.

4 Melt 25g/1oz of the butter in a clean saucepan and cook the chopped shallots for 5–6 minutes until very soft. Add half the cooked lentils and put aside. Put the remaining lentils into a blender or food processor with 150ml/1/4 pint of the cooking liquid and blend to a purée. With the motor still running, add the remaining 50g/2oz of butter until smooth. Stir into the whole lentils and shallots and season very well. Put aside.

5 Barbecue the duck breasts, skin side down, over Direct Low heat for 7–8 minutes, until the skin is golden brown. Turn over and cook for a further 3–4 minutes, until they are just firm to the touch. Add another 2 minutes cooking time on each side for more well done. If there is a flare-up during cooking, move the duck to a cooler part of the grill for a minute to let the flames subside, then continue cooking.

6 Reheat the lentils and spoon on to a large platter. Top with the duck breasts and garnish with sprigs of rosemary.

Chilli-glazed poussin with grilled sweet potatoes

main course: serves 4	**gas:** indirect & direct / medium heat	**charcoal:** indirect	**prep time:** 10 mins + marinating	**barbecue time:** 1 hour

Homemade harissa gives a really good fresh flavour to this dish but you can use commercially ready-made if you want to cut corners. The sweetness of the potato complements the heat of the harissa.

4 poussins

salt

freshly ground black pepper

6 tablespoons Harissa (page 21)

900g/2lb medium-sized sweet potatoes, unpeeled

4 tablespoons olive oil

1 Put the poussins into a large shallow dish. Season well and spoon a little of the harissa into the cavity of each bird. Use a pastry brush to spread it right over the birds and into all the nooks and crannies. Cover loosely with cling film and put in the refrigerator to marinate for at least 2 hours.

2 Brush each poussin with oil and season them with salt. Barbecue over Indirect Medium heat for 40–45 minutes, until the juices run clear when the thickest part of the thigh is pierced with a knife.

3 Shortly before the chicken is going to be fully cooked, cut the sweet potatoes into 1.5cm/$1/2$ inch slices. Put into a large bowl and toss with the olive oil and a little salt.

4 Put the cooked birds on a platter and cover with foil to keep warm. Barbecue the potato slices over Direct Medium heat for 10–12 minutes, turning once, until tender and slightly charred. You can pop the birds back onto the barbecue with the potatoes for 1 minute, if they have cooled too much.

5 Serve the poussins and the sweet potato with extra harissa.

Goose with apple sauce & walnuts

main course: serves 4–6	gas: indirect / medium heat	charcoal: indirect	prep time: 20 mins	barbecue time: 3 hours

Geese are very fatty birds to cook, so it's important to drain off the huge amount of fat that's emitted from the goose at least 2 or 3 times during barbecuing, to avoid it overspilling and catching fire.

4.5–5.5kg/10–12lb oven-ready goose

salt

freshly ground black pepper

2 oranges

few large sprigs of fresh thyme

Apple sauce

100g/4oz dried apples, roughly chopped

2 oranges, juice only

3 tablespoons Calvados (apple brandy)

50g/2oz walnuts, roughly chopped

1 Season the cavity of the goose. Cut the oranges in half and put into the cavity, together with the sprigs of thyme. Prick the skin all over with a skewer to help release the fat and season. Cover the legs and wings of the goose with foil. Sit on a wire rack set in a large heavy-duty foil pan or roasting tin.

2 Barbecue over Indirect Medium heat for $2^3/_4$–3 hours, draining off the fat from the foil pan or roasting tray every 30 minutes.

3 While the goose is cooking, make the apple sauce: Put the chopped dried apples into a medium-sized saucepan with 350ml/12fl oz water. Cover and bring to the boil. Reduce the heat and simmer for 20–25 minutes until very soft. Uncover and boil off any remaining water. Put into a food processor with the orange juice and Calvados and blend until smooth. Stir in the walnuts.

4 Remove the goose from the barbecue. Drain off any fat in the tin. Remove the foil from the wings and legs. Cover with foil and leave to rest for 15 minutes before serving with the warm apple and walnut sauce.

Grilled quail
with cumin dipping salt

main course: serves 4	gas: indirect / medium heat	charcoal: indirect	prep time: 25 mins + marinating	barbecue time: 20 mins

For this dish, grinding your own cumin seeds is a must. The cumin seeds are toasted to release their flavour, then ground to a powder using a mortar and pestle.

8 oven-ready quails, each weighing 100–150g/4–5oz

2 tablespoons cumin seeds

3 tablespoons extra virgin olive oil

salt

freshly ground black pepper

Cumin dipping salt

1 plump garlic clove, finely chopped

4 tablespoons fresh coriander, roughly chopped

1 lemon, grated zest only

1 tablespoon coarse sea salt

1 Spatchcock the quails (see pages 72–73) and put aside.

2 Put the cumin seeds into a clean frying pan and place over a high heat for a few seconds until their aroma rises. Remove from the heat and grind finely using a mortar and pestle.

3 Put 1 tablespoon of the ground cumin into a small bowl and mix with the olive oil to form a paste. Use to brush all over the quails. Season and cover and leave to marinate in the refrigerator for 30 minutes.

4 Barbecue the marinated quails over Indirect Medium heat for 15–20 minutes, turning once until tender and the juices run clear.

5 Meanwhile, to make the cumin dipping salt: Mix the remaining 1 tablespoon of ground cumin, garlic, coriander, lemon zest and sea salt together in a small bowl. Serve 2 quails per person with a little of this dipping mixture on the side.

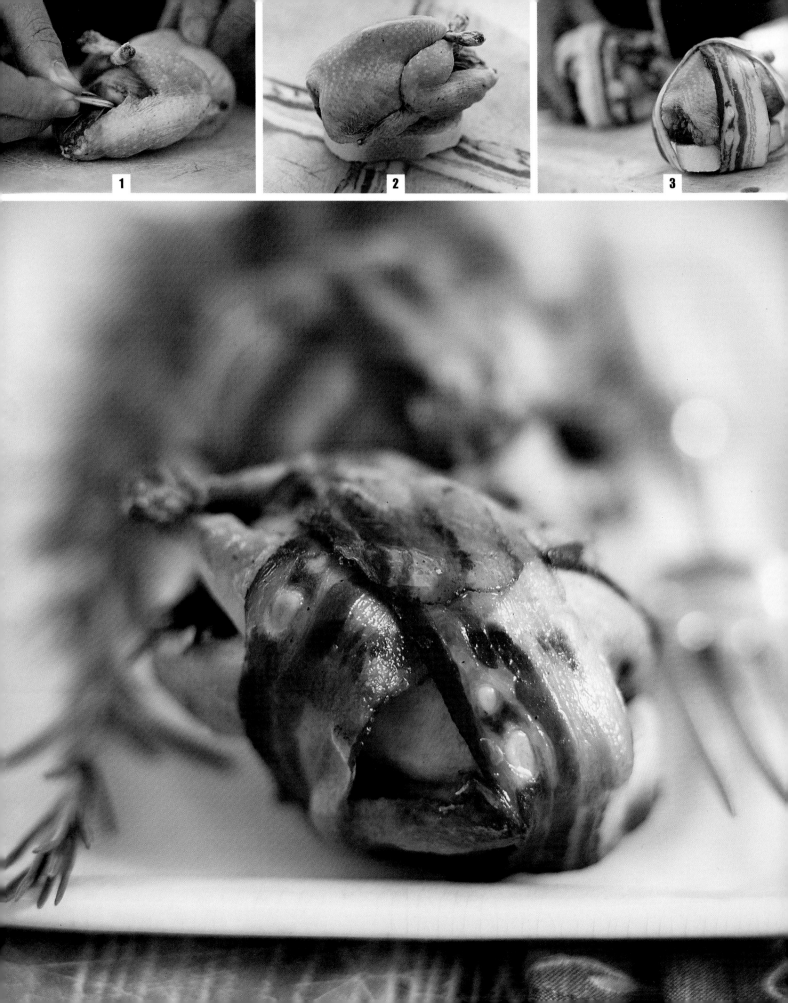

Glazed quail pancetta parcels

main course: serves 4	gas: direct & indirect / medium heat	charcoal: direct & indirect	prep time: 15 mins	barbecue time: 30 mins

In Italy, pancetta is used to flavour meats, and it is especially good at keeping game from drying out if wrapped round it. The bread soaks up the juices from the birds as they cook. In this recipe, baguette or ciabatta may be used, just make sure the slices are roughly the same size as the quails.

8 oven-ready quails, each weighing 100–150g/4–5oz

8 small sprigs of fresh rosemary

salt

freshly ground black pepper

16 slices of pancetta or very thin streaky bacon

8 slices of baguette, about 1.5cm/¹⁄₂ inch thick

Glaze

2 tablespoons olive oil

1 plump garlic clove, crushed

¹⁄₂ lemon, juice only

1 tablespoon fresh flat leaf parsley, chopped

2 tablespoons Marsala (or Madeira)

1 tablespoon clear honey

1 Remove and discard the livers from inside the quails, if necessary. **1** Pop a sprig of rosemary inside each quail and season well inside and out. **2** Lay a slice of pancetta on a clean surface and top with another slice to form a cross. Place a slice of baguette in the middle. Top the baguette with a quail and **3** wrap the quail in the pancetta like a parcel, making sure the ends of the pancetta overlap. Repeat with the remaining pancetta, baguette slices and quails. Put aside.

2 To make the glaze: Put the olive oil, garlic, lemon juice, parsley, Marsala, honey and plenty of seasoning in a medium-sized bowl and mix together well. Put aside.

3 Barbecue the quail over Direct Medium heat for 5 minutes, turning once, to sear all over. Continue barbecuing over Indirect Medium heat for 20–25 minutes, brushing with the glaze every 5 minutes and turning once, until the pancetta is golden and the juices run clear.

4 Serve two quails per person.

meat on the grill

Lamb rosettes with anchovy, pancetta & garlic

main course: serves 4	gas: direct / medium heat	charcoal: direct	prep time: 35 mins	barbecue time: 10 mins

Matching the saltiness of anchovies with meat is a favourite trick of the Italians. Here the anchovies, pancetta, garlic and parsley form a wonderful pungent paste that becomes a secret flavour in the middle of each cutlet.

50g/2oz wafer-thin slice of pancetta

6 anchovy fillets in olive oil, drained

2 tablespoons fresh parsley, chopped

2 plump garlic cloves, crushed

1 tablespoon balsamic vinegar

8 large loin lamb chops

olive oil, for brushing

salt

freshly ground black pepper

Italian bean salad (page 179), to serve

1 Put the pancetta, anchovy fillets, parsley, garlic and vinegar into a food processor and blend until they form a paste. Put aside.

2 To make the rosettes: Trim off any excess thick fat from the lamb chops, leaving a thin layer of fat. **1** Carefully cut around the bone in each chop and remove. You should now have a nice eye of meat with a long thin flap. Make an incision in the side of the eye of meat, to form a pocket in each chop. **2** Fill each with a little of the pancetta and anchovy paste. **3** Wrap the flap around the eye of meat and secure with a small skewer or cocktail stick (if using wooden cocktail sticks, soak them in cold water for at least 30 minutes first).

3 Brush the lamb rosettes with a little oil and season well. Barbecue the chops over Direct Medium heat for 8–10 minutes, turning once. Add an extra 1–2 minutes of cooking time on each side if you prefer the lamb well done. Serve with an Italian bean salad.

Coriander-spiced lamb fillets with lemon tahini sauce

main course: serves 6	gas: direct / medium heat	charcoal: direct	prep time: 20 mins + marinating	barbecue time: 10 mins

The flavour of this Greek recipe is influenced by the neighbouring Middle East. The recipe uses lamb fillet, but you can also use lamb neck fillet which, while slightly more fatty, has excellent flavour and is much more economical.

2 plump garlic cloves, crushed

1 shallot, finely chopped

1 1/2 teaspoons ground coriander

1/2 teaspoon ground cumin

1/2 teaspoon ground allspice

1/4 teaspoon dried oregano

1 lemon, juice only

2 tablespoons olive oil

1 teaspoon sun-dried tomato paste

salt

freshly ground black pepper

450g/1lb lamb fillet

Lemon tahini sauce

1 plump garlic clove, crushed

7 tablespoons tahini paste

1 lemon, juice only

lemon wedges, to serve

1 Put the garlic cloves, shallot, the ground coriander, cumin, allspice, oregano, 2 tablespoons of lemon juice, the olive oil, tomato paste and seasoning into a small food processor or blender and blend to give a thick paste. Scrape the paste into a large bowl.

2 Trim the lamb and cut into 4cm/1 1/2 inch dice. Stir the diced lamb into the paste until the lamb is well coated. Cover and put into the refrigerator to marinate for at least 2 hours. If using wooden or bamboo skewers, soak 4 in cold water for at least 30 minutes.

3 Meanwhile to make the sauce: Put the garlic, tahini and lemon juice into a bowl and whisk until smooth. Whisk in 85ml/3fl oz water and season. Cover and leave for at least 30 minutes before using, to let the flavours develop.

4 Thread the lamb on 4 skewers and season with a little salt and pepper. Barbecue the lamb over Direct Medium heat for 8–10 minutes, turning once, until tender but still slightly pink inside. Serve hot with the lemon tahini sauce and lemon wedges.

Spiced leg of lamb
with mint & chilli relish

main course: serves 6	gas: direct / medium heat	charcoal: direct	prep time: 20 mins + marinating	barbecue time: 30 mins

This lamb dish needs to marinate overnight as the marinade is made of yoghurt and spices that are mild and fragrant. It is served with a sweet and hot relish of fresh chopped mint and chilli.

1 teaspoon cumin seeds

large pinch of saffron strands

2 plump garlic cloves, crushed

4 teaspoons Harissa (page 21)

$\frac{1}{2}$ lemon, juice only

1 shallot, very finely chopped

200g/7oz Greek yoghurt

$\frac{1}{2}$ teaspoon salt

1.5kg/3–3$\frac{1}{2}$lb leg of lamb, boned

Mint & chilli relish

1 teaspoon caster sugar

2 tablespoons lemon juice

6 tablespoons fresh mint, chopped

1 small red chilli, deseeded and very finely chopped

6 tablespoons extra virgin olive oil

salt

freshly ground black pepper

1 The day before, put the cumin seeds into a small clean pan and put over a high heat until their aroma rises. Remove from the heat and roughly crush using a mortar and pestle. Transfer to a large bowl. Soak the saffron in 2 tablespoons of boiling water for 10 minutes. To the cumin add the saffron, garlic, chilli sauce, lemon juice, shallot, yoghurt and salt, and stir very well. Put aside.

2 Open out the boned leg of lamb on a clean surface. Trim off any excess fat. Cut the lamb into 2 or 3 sections, so you can start barbecuing the thickest piece first, finishing with the thinnest. Make a few deep slashes in the flesh-side of the meat and put the lamb in a large flat shallow dish. Pour over the yoghurt marinade and use a brush to work it well into the slashes. Cover loosely with cling film and put in the refrigerator to marinate overnight.

3 An hour before you want to cook the lamb, make the relish. Put the caster sugar into a small bowl and pour over the lemon juice. Stir until dissolved. Stir in the chopped mint, chilli, olive oil and seasoning. Leave at room temperature to let the flavours develop.

4 Season the lamb and barbecue the thickest piece first over Direct Medium heat. Pieces over 5cm/2 inches thick will take 25–35 minutes to cook; pieces 2.5–5cm/1–2 inches thick will take 15–20 minutes. Turn all the pieces halfway through the cooking time. If you like your lamb rare, reduce all the times by about 5 minutes. Leave the cooked lamb to rest for 5 minutes before slicing. Serve with the mint and chilli relish.

Barbecued lamb greek style

| main course: serves 6–8 | gas: indirect / medium heat | charcoal: indirect | prep time: 40 mins | barbecue time: 1½ hours |

Every island, every village and every mother in Greece will have their own recipe for stuffing and cooking the lamb at Easter, one of the most important events in the Greek calendar. This version uses rice, spinach and mint for the stuffing. Traditionally the lamb is cooked until fairly well done, so if you prefer it pink reduce the cooking time slightly.

1.75kg/4–4½lb leg of lamb, boned

Stuffing

50g/2oz long-grain rice

3 tablespoons olive oil

50g/2oz lamb's liver, rinsed and chopped

2 bunches of spring onions, roughly chopped

½ teaspoon sweet paprika

225g/8oz fresh leaf spinach

3 tablespoons fresh mint, chopped

salt

freshly ground black pepper

oil, for brushing

4 lemons

fresh mint, to garnish

1 To prepare the lamb for stuffing, open out the boned leg on a clean surface and trim off any excess fat. **1** Hold the knife so the blade is lying flat on the meat and slice horizontally into the thickest part of the meat, then open out the meat like a flap. Repeat in 2 or 3 places where the meat is quite thick.

2 To make the stuffing: Cook the rice according to packet instructions until just tender. Drain well and refresh under cold water. Drain again and put into a large bowl. Heat 2 tablespoons of the olive oil in a large saucepan and cook the chopped liver for 1 minute. Add the spring onions and cook for a further 2–3 minutes, until they are wilted. Stir in the paprika and cook for a further 1 minute.

3 Wash and dry the spinach. Heat the remaining 1 tablespoon of oil in the pan and cook the spinach for 1–2 minutes until just wilted. Tip into a colander and press out any excess liquid. Coarsely chop. Add to the liver, spring onion mixture with the rice, mint and seasoning and combine well.

4 Open out the flaps you have made in the meat. **2** Spread the stuffing all over the lamb and fold the flaps back over. Don't worry if some of the stuffing is still uncovered, as you will be rolling up the meat. **3** Roll the meat lengthwise. **4** Tie as tightly as possible in 7 or 8 places.

5 Brush the lamb all over with oil and season with salt and pepper. Barbecue the stuffed, rolled joint over Indirect Medium heat for 1–1½ hours, turning once. Add an extra 10–15 minutes for meat

that is more well done. Remove the lamb and leave to rest for 10 minutes before carving. Cut the lemons in half, place cut side down on the cooking grate and sear over Direct Medium heat for about 5 minutes, until slightly charred.

6 Slice the lamb and arrange on a large platter. Garnish with the charred lemons and fresh bunches of mint.

Souvlakia

main course: serves 6	gas: direct / high heat	charcoal: direct	prep time: 30 mins + chilling	barbecue time: 8 mins

Souvlakia shops exist all over Greece and are to the Greeks what burger joints are to the Americans. These kebabs of lamb can, however, also be made with minced veal or pork. They are always cooked over a barbecue and served wrapped in bread with salad. This recipe is a great main course or will otherwise serve 12 as a delicious snack.

900g/2lb finely minced lamb

1 onion, finely chopped

6 tablespoons fresh flat leaf parsley, chopped

2 tablespoons fresh mint, chopped

2 teaspoons ground cumin

salt

freshly ground black pepper

oil, for brushing

Salad

1 cos lettuce

1 bunch of spring onions

3 tablespoons fresh dill, chopped

4 tomatoes, cut into wedges

extra virgin olive oil

6 pitta or Middle-Eastern flat breads

1 lemon, cut into wedges

1 If using wooden or bamboo skewers, soak 12 in cold water for at least 30 minutes.

2 Put the minced lamb, onion, parsley, mint and cumin into a large bowl. Season well and mix thoroughly, using your hands.

3 Divide the mixture into 12 equal portions and roll each into a rough sausage shape, about 12.5cm/5 inches long. Mould each piece around a skewer and press into shape until about 15–18cm/ 6–7 inches long. Put on a plate and chill in the refrigerator for 30 minutes to firm up.

4 Brush the kebabs with a little oil, and barbecue over Direct High heat for 6–8 minutes, turning once until the lamb is cooked through.

5 While the lamb is cooking, make the salad: Shred the lettuce finely and put into a large bowl. Finely chop the spring onions and add to the lettuce. Add the dill and the tomato wedges, and drizzle with extra virgin olive oil. Season well and toss everything together.

6 Warm the pitta or flat breads for 1–2 minutes on the barbecue. If using pitta breads, split and fill with the salad and arrange the kebabs on top. Serve with lemon wedges.

Grilled lamb & vegetables with fresh plum tomato dressing

| main course: serves 4 | gas: direct / medium heat | charcoal: direct | prep time: 30 mins + marinating | barbecue time: 12 mins |

Ratatouille, the classic vegetable dish from Provence, has been given the barbecue treatment by grilling the quintessential vegetables and using the traditional seasoning and flavourings as a marinade.

675g/1½lb lamb neck fillet

2 plump garlic cloves, crushed

1 tablespoon sun-dried tomato paste

1 tablespoon fresh oregano, chopped

6 tablespoons olive oil

salt

freshly ground black pepper

1 large aubergine

1 large onion

2 courgettes

2 red peppers

plenty of oil, for brushing

Plum tomato dressing

2 ripe plum tomatoes, skinned, deseeded and finely diced

5 tablespoons extra virgin olive oil

2 tablespoons red wine vinegar

2 tablespoons fresh basil, chopped

fresh basil sprigs, to garnish

green salad, to serve

1 Trim the excess fat from the lamb, cut into bite-size pieces and put into a bowl. In a small bowl toss together the garlic, tomato paste, oregano, olive oil and seasoning. Pour over the lamb. Cover and leave in the refrigerator for 1 hour to marinate.

2 Trim off the ends from the aubergine and cut the rest into 1.5cm/½ inch thick slices. Cut the onion into 1.5cm/½ inch slices. Trim off the ends from the courgettes and slice 1.5cm/½ inch thick. Halve the peppers, deseed and cut into quarters.

3 Brush all the vegetable pieces generously with oil. Arrange over Direct Medium heat, leaving room for the lamb skewers, and barbecue for 2 minutes. Remove the lamb from the bowl and pour the marinade into a small saucepan. Boil for 1 full minute, then remove from the heat and set aside. Skewer the lamb on a few long metal skewers (it doesn't matter how many, you won't be serving the lamb on the skewers). Put on the barbecue with the vegetables and barbecue both for a further 8–10 minutes, turning once and brushing with the reserved marinade for the last 2 minutes.

4 While the vegetables and lamb are cooking, make the dressing: Put the diced tomato, olive oil, red wine vinegar, basil and plenty of seasoning in a small clean bowl and mix well.

5 Remove all the food from the grill and put on a large platter. Remove the pieces of lamb from the skewers using a fork and toss them with the vegetables. Drizzle over the dressing and garnish with basil sprigs. Serve warm with a crisp green salad.

Spinach-stuffed veal chops with gremolada

main course: serves 4	gas: direct / medium heat	charcoal: direct	prep time: 25 mins	barbecue time: 16 mins

Gremolada is a flavouring of fresh parsley, chopped garlic and grated lemon zest that comes from Milan and is most often paired with veal, as in *osso buco*. It is always sprinkled over, or added, at the end of cooking just before serving.

25g/1oz butter

2 plump garlic cloves, crushed

1 shallot, very finely chopped

1 tablespoon olive oil

175g/6oz baby spinach leaves

25g/1oz Parmesan cheese, coarsely grated

salt

freshly ground black pepper

Gremolada

2 plump garlic cloves, finely chopped

2 tablespoons fresh flat leaf parsley, finely chopped

1 lemon, finely grated zest only

4 thick veal chops, each about 2.5cm/1 inch thick

oil, for brushing

1 Melt the butter in a small saucepan and add the crushed garlic and the chopped shallot, and cook gently for 3–4 minutes until softened. Heat the olive oil in a large pan, and add the spinach leaves, cooking gently until just wilted. Remove from the heat and drain well, pressing out any excess water. Turn out onto a chopping board and chop roughly. Put the sautéed garlic and shallots with the spinach into a medium-sized bowl, add the Parmesan, season and stir together well. Put aside.

2 To make the gremolada: Put the chopped garlic, chopped parsley and grated lemon zest into a small bowl. Mix well and put aside.

3 Using a sharp-pointed knife, make a deep incision in the side of the veal chops, to form deep pockets. Divide the spinach stuffing into 4 and use to stuff each chop, pushing the stuffing in as far as possible. Secure with a cocktail stick (if using wooden cocktails sticks soak in cold water for at least 30 minutes first).

4 Brush the chops with a little oil and season with salt and pepper. Barbecue the chops over Direct Medium heat for 14–16 minutes, turning once during cooking, until tender but still slightly pink in the middle.

5 Remove the chops from the grill, put on 4 plates, and sprinkle a little of the gremolada over each.

Veal chops stuffed with sage & prosciutto

main course: serves 4	gas: direct / medium heat	charcoal: direct	prep time: 15 mins	barbecue time: 16 mins

Saltimbocca is a classic Italian dish of thin slices of veal and ham sandwiched together with sage, then rolled up and pan-fried. Here is an equally delicious version created especially for the barbecue.

50g/2oz prosciutto

2 lemons, grated zest and juice

2 tablespoons fresh sage leaves, roughly chopped

salt

freshly ground black pepper

4 thick veal chops, each about 2.5cm/1 inch thick

oil, for brushing

25g/1oz unsalted butter, chilled and cut into 4 slices

4 fresh sage sprigs, to garnish

1 Put the prosciutto into a food processor. Add all the zest from both lemons and just 1 tablespoon of juice squeezed from 1 lemon. Reserve the other lemon. Add the chopped sage and seasoning, and blend to a roughly chopped paste.

2 Pat the veal chops dry with kitchen paper. Make 4 deep slashes in the top of each chop, cutting about three-quarters of the way through. Push the paste down into the slashes.

3 Brush the chops with a little oil and season lightly with salt and pepper. Barbecue the chops, paste side down first, over Direct Medium heat for 14–16 minutes, turning once halfway through cooking, until tender but still slightly pink in the middle.

4 Remove the veal chops from the barbecue and put on 4 plates. Top each with a slice of butter. Cut the reserved lemon in half and squeeze a splash of juice over the butter and veal. Garnish with sage sprigs.

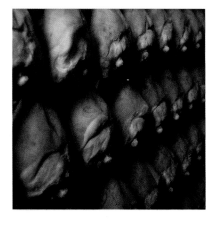

DID YOU KNOW? The Italian ham, prosciutto, is renowned for its delicate flavour. The Italians achieve this by feeding the pigs the whey left over from making Parmesan cheese.

Wine-marinated rabbit
with fig & prune chutney

main course: serves 4	gas: direct & indirect / high & medium heat	charcoal: direct & indirect	prep time: 15 mins + marinating	barbecue time: 25 mins

This recipe combines figs with rabbit, both common to most Mediterranean countries. Farmed and wild rabbit are both available nowadays. For the barbecue you should buy reared rabbit, as wild rabbit needs slower, gentler cooking.

600ml/1 pint fruity red wine

2 plump garlic cloves, crushed

1 onion, roughly chopped

1 carrot, roughly diced

1 celery stalk, sliced

1 bay leaf

1 sprig of fresh thyme

few parsley stalks

salt

freshly ground black pepper

1 rabbit, jointed into 6 pieces

4 tablespoons olive oil

oil, for brushing

Easy fig and prune chutney, to serve (page 22)

1 The day before, put the red wine, garlic, onion, carrot, celery, bay leaf, thyme sprig and parsley stalks into a large shallow bowl, season and mix well. Add the rabbit pieces and toss in the marinade. Leave to marinate overnight in the refrigerator.

2 Remove the rabbit pieces from the wine marinade. Strain off 2–3 tablespoons of the marinade into a bowl. Add the olive oil, season and mix well. Brush this over the rabbit pieces. Discard any leftover marinade.

3 Barbecue the rabbit over Direct High heat for 5 minutes, turning once. Continue barbecuing over Indirect Medium heat for 15–20 minutes, turning once until tender and no longer pink in the centre.

4 Serve the rabbit with the fig and prune chutney.

Rabbit stuffed with chillies & olives

| **main course:** serves 4 | **gas:** direct & indirect / medium heat | **charcoal:** direct | **prep time:** 35 mins + marinating | **barbecue time:** 25 mins |

This recipe uses Spanish olives to provide a salty stuffing and Catalan Romesco sauce to give a spicy complement to the meat. The meatiest part of the rabbit leg is the thigh, so you may find the joint referred to as either leg or thigh depending on where you shop. Either way it's a delicious tender joint that's easy to bone out and stuff.

50g/2oz green olives, pitted and roughly chopped

1 plump garlic clove, crushed

1 red chilli, deseeded and finely chopped

2 tablespoons fresh parsley, chopped

1 tablespoon fresh tarragon, chopped

salt

freshly ground black pepper

4 rabbit legs

150ml/¼ pint white wine

150ml/¼ pint olive oil

Romesco sauce (page 21), to serve

1 Put the chopped olives, garlic, chilli, parsley and the tarragon into a small bowl. Season and mix well. Put aside.

2 Take the rabbit legs and cut along the line of the bone, to expose it. **1** Scrape away the meat from the bone, then completely cut out the bone and discard. Open out the boned legs and divide the stuffing between each. **2** Fold over to form parcels and encase the stuffing. **3** Secure with cocktail sticks (if using wooden cocktail sticks, soak them in cold water for at least 30 minutes first).

3 Mix the white wine and olive oil together and season well. Pour over the rabbit parcels and marinate in the refrigerator for 2 hours, turning occasionally.

4 Season the rabbit parcels with salt and pepper and barbecue them over Direct Medium heat for 5 minutes, turning once. Continue barbecuing the parcels over Indirect Medium heat for 15–20 minutes, turning once until tender and the meat is no longer pink in the centre.

5 Serve with Romesco sauce on the side.

Merguez sausage with roasted beetroot & yoghurt dressing

main course: serves 4	gas: direct / medium heat	charcoal: direct	prep time: 1 hour	barbecue time: 12 mins

Merguez is a spicy, Moroccan sausage. You could also use chorizo sausages, as long as they are the raw variety made for cooking and not the cured type. The beetroot dressing adds a cool flavour to the spiciness of the sausage.

450g/1lb fresh beetroot

1 plump garlic clove, crushed

200g/7oz Greek yoghurt

1 lemon, juice only

salt

freshly ground black pepper

2 tablespoons fresh parsley, chopped

8 merguez sausages

oil, for brushing

4 Middle-Eastern flat breads or large pitta breads

handful of rocket leaves

1 Trim the beetroot, rinse and put into a saucepan. Cover with cold water and bring to the boil. Simmer for 30 minutes to 1 hour, depending on how big they are. They are done when you can slip the tip of a knife easily into them, like cooked potatoes. Drain well and rub away the skins under cold running water. Drain and pat dry on kitchen paper. Put aside.

2 Put the garlic, yoghurt, lemon juice and seasoning into a large bowl, and mix well. Cut the beetroot into small dice and add to the bowl with the parsley. Fold everything together and put aside.

3 Brush the merguez sausages with a little oil, and barbecue them over Direct Medium heat for 6–8 minutes, turning once. If the sausages begin to flare up, move to Indirect heat for the last 5–6 minutes of cooking.

4 Put the sausages aside and keep warm. Put the flat breads on the barbecue for 2–3 minutes to heat through.

5 Serve a spoonful of the beetroot dressing in a flat bread with a few rocket leaves and a couple of merguez sausages.

Grilled minced beef kebabs with tagine sauce

| main course: serves 4 | gas: direct / medium heat | charcoal: direct | prep time: 30 mins + chilling | barbecue time: 10 mins |

A tagine is a Moroccan clay pot in which meat and vegetables are cooked slowly together. *Kefta* is minced meat (lamb or beef), liberally spiced. Shaped and skewered here, to make it easy to cook on the barbecue, it is served with a tagine-style sauce.

450g/1lb minced beef

1 teaspoon salt

$1/4$ teaspoon freshly ground black pepper

1 small onion, very finely chopped

1 teaspoon ground cumin

2 teaspoons paprika

3 tablespoons fresh parsley, chopped

Tagine sauce

large pinch of saffron strands

50g/2oz unsalted butter

1 onion, very finely chopped

1 level teaspoon ground ginger

$1/4$ teaspoon freshly ground black pepper

$1/2$ teaspoon cayenne pepper

4 tablespoons fresh coriander, chopped

1 lemon, juice only

oil, for brushing

Broad bean, pea and mint couscous, to serve (page 177)

Harissa (page 21), to serve

1 Put the minced beef, salt, pepper, onion, cumin, paprika and parsley into a large bowl and mix very well. You may find this easier to do using your hands. Divide the mixture into 8 portions. Take each piece and shape into a sausage about 7.5cm/3 inches long. Put on a plate and chill for 30 minutes to help firm up. If using wooden or bamboo skewers, soak 4 long skewers in cold water for at least 30 minutes.

2 Meanwhile, to make the tagine sauce: Grind the saffron to a fine powder using a mortar and pestle and put aside. Melt the butter in a small saucepan, add the onion and cook for 4–5 minutes until softened. Add the saffron, ginger, pepper, cayenne pepper and coriander and cook for 1 minute. Add 300ml/$1/2$ pint of water and 2 tablespoons of lemon juice and bring to the boil. Reduce the heat and simmer gently, uncovered, for 15–20 minutes.

3 Thread a skewer lengthwise through 2 *kefta* and gently squeeze the meat on to the skewers, so you have 2 sausage shapes on each skewer. Brush each filled skewer with oil, and barbecue over Direct Medium heat for 8–10 minutes, turning once, until cooked through.

4 Meanwhile, make the broad bean, pea and mint couscous and spoon a pile on to a platter. Spoon the hot sauce around it and sit the *kefta* on top. Serve some harissa on the side if you like.

Barbecued beef, gherkin & new potato salad

main course: serves 4	**gas:** direct / medium heat	**charcoal:** direct	**prep time:** 35 mins + cooling	**barbecue time:** 16 mins

For this delicious warm salad, popular in France, use the tiny pickled gherkins known as *cornichons*, which have a wonderful sweet nutty flavour that won't overpower the mild horseradish and mustard flavour of the warm beef. This makes a wonderful alternative to Sunday roast in the summer months.

675g/1½lb waxy new potatoes, such as Pink Fir Apple or Charlotte

Vinaigrette dressing

6 tablespoons extra virgin olive oil

2 tablespoons red wine vinegar

good pinch of sugar

salt

freshly ground black pepper

1 small red onion, thinly sliced

250g/9oz plum cherry tomatoes, halved

3 tablespoons extra virgin live oil

2 teaspoons grated horseradish (either fresh or from a jar)

1 teaspoon Dijon mustard

675g/1½lb piece of beef fillet or sirloin

4 little gem lettuces

20 small pickled gherkins (*cornichons*), cut in half lengthways

1 Put the potatoes into a pan of cold salted water. Bring to the boil, reduce the heat and simmer for 15–20 minutes, until tender. Drain well.

2 Meanwhile, to make the vinaigrette: Whisk the olive oil, red wine vinegar, sugar and some seasoning together.

3 While still hot, cut the drained potatoes into quarters, put in a large bowl and leave to cool. Then add the sliced red onion, cherry tomatoes and pour over the vinaigrette and leave for about 1 hour to let the flavours develop.

4 Mix the olive oil with the horseradish, mustard and seasoning, and put aside. Brush the beef with a little of the horseradish mixture.

5 Barbecue the beef over Direct Medium heat for 8–10 minutes, turning once and brushing again with the horseradish mixture. Brush with more horseradish mixture and barbecue for a further 2–3 minutes. Turn and brush again and barbecue for a final 2–3 minutes. Add an extra 5–8 minutes for well done. Leave to rest for 10 minutes before slicing.

6 Separate the lettuce into leaves and tear roughly. Put them in a large bowl and spoon over the potato, tomato and vinaigrette mixture. Scatter with the halved gherkins. Cut the meat into slices and toss through the salad. Serve while the meat is still warm, either as a single serving or on a large serving platter.

Seared steaks & potatoes with salmoriglio

main course: serves 4	gas: direct / medium heat	charcoal: direct	prep time: 15 mins	barbecue time: 12 mins

Italian cooks are famous for their variety of herb mixtures used to flavour meat. This salmoriglio mixture – an intensely flavoured, no-cook herb sauce – is used here to dress warm steaks fresh from the grill.

900g/2lb large potatoes, such as Maris Piper or King Edward

olive oil

salt

freshly ground black pepper

4 sirloin beef steaks, each weighing 225–350g/8–12oz

Salmoriglio, **to serve (page 22)**

Rocket and Parmesan salad (page 177), to serve

1 Peel the potatoes and cut into slices about 1.5cm/$\frac{1}{2}$ inch thick. Put into a large bowl, sprinkle over some oil and plenty of seasoning, and toss well until coated all over. Arrange the potatoes over Direct Medium heat, leaving plenty of room for the 4 steaks, and cook for 2 minutes. Brush the steaks with oil, season with salt and pepper and cook for 8–10 minutes, turning the steaks and potatoes once. Cook the steaks for an extra 1–2 minutes for well done.

2 Arrange the steaks on a platter and surround with the potatoes. Spoon the salmoriglio dressing over the steaks. Serve with a rocket and Parmesan salad.

Grilled steaks & mushrooms with roquefort sauce

main course: serves 4	gas: direct / medium heat	charcoal: direct	prep time: 15 mins	barbecue time: 25 mins

The celebrated French blue cheese, Roquefort, is matured for up to a year in the cool limestone caves in the tiny village of Roquefort-sur-Soulzon. In this recipe it is melted to make a delicious sauce to serve with grilled steak and mushrooms.

Roquefort sauce

25g/1oz butter

1 shallot, finely chopped

1 plump garlic clove, crushed

225g/8oz Roquefort cheese

4 tablespoons crème fraîche

2 tablespoons fresh parsley, chopped

6 tablespoons olive oil

1 teaspoon fresh rosemary, chopped

1 teaspoon fresh thyme, chopped

4 very large field or portobello mushrooms (measuring 12.5cm/ 5 inches across), stems removed

salt

freshly ground black pepper

4 beef fillet steaks, each weighing about 175g–200g/6–7oz

1 To make the Roquefort sauce: Melt the butter in a small saucepan. Add the shallot and garlic, and cook for 3–4 minutes until softened. Break the Roquefort into pieces and whisk into the sauce over a gentle heat until all the cheese has melted. Stir in the crème fraîche until smooth, then stir in the parsley and put aside.

2 Mix the olive oil with the rosemary and thyme. Brush over the cup side of the mushrooms and season. Barbecue the mushrooms over Direct Medium heat for 12–15 minutes, turning once and brushing with more oil halfway through cooking. Keep the mushrooms warm.

3 Brush the steaks with the remaining herb oil, season and barbecue over Direct Medium heat for 8–10 minutes, turning once. Add an extra 1–2 minutes each side for well done.

4 Warm the sauce through. Put a steak on top of each mushroom, spoon over the sauce and serve.

Garlic & mustard steaks in baguettes

| **light lunch:** serves 4 | **gas:** direct / high heat | **charcoal:** direct | **prep time:** 10 mins | **barbecue time:** 8 mins |

Nothing beats succulent grilled steaks hot from the barbecue, slowly dripping flavour and juices into a fresh crusty baguette. Here, the spiciness of a good French Dijon mustard combined with the crunch of crisp watercress adds a Gallic touch to a classic steak sandwich.

3 plump garlic cloves, crushed

1 tablespoon olive oil

2 teaspoons sun-dried tomato paste

1 teaspoon Tabasco sauce

1 tablespoon white wine vinegar

2 tablespoons Dijon mustard

2 tablespoons wholegrain Dijon mustard

4 tablespoons runny honey

salt

freshly ground black pepper

4 sirloin beef steaks, each weighing 100–175g/4–6oz

1 large baguette

4 tablespoons mayonnaise

handful of watercress

1 Put the garlic, olive oil, tomato paste, Tabasco, vinegar, both mustards and honey into a bowl, and beat together until thoroughly mixed. Season well and mix again. Put aside.

2 Trim the steaks of any excess fat. Put each steak between sheets of cling film and bat out to half its original thickness. Brush the garlic and mustard mixture over both sides of each steak.

3 Barbecue the steaks over Direct High heat for 4–6 minutes, turning once and brushing with the mustard mixture once more (use a clean basting brush). Remove from the barbecue and keep warm.

4 Cut the baguette into 4 even-sized pieces. Split each piece open lenghways and open out like a book. Barbecue over Direct High heat for 1–2 minutes until toasted and marked by the grill.

5 Quickly spread the toasted side of each piece of bread with mayonnaise and partly close up again. Put a steak into each one, folding or cutting the steak to fit, and finish with watercress.

Venison steaks with sweet redcurrant butter

main course: serves 6	gas: direct / medium heat	charcoal: direct	prep time: 20 mins + marinating	barbecue time: 8 mins

Juniper berries and redcurrants give contrasting flavours of sweet and savoury to this dish. Venison meat is dense, fine-textured and very lean, and needs to be brushed well with oil and cooked quickly to prevent it from drying out. Unless you are used to cooking wild meat, farmed venison is a safer bet as it is much more tender.

Marinade

1 shallot, chopped

1 plump garlic clove, chopped

4 juniper berries, crushed

1 bay leaf

1 sprig of fresh rosemary

150ml/$\frac{1}{4}$ pint fruity red wine

75ml/$\frac{1}{2}$ pint olive oil

salt

freshly ground black pepper

6 venison steaks, each weighing about 200–250g/7–9oz

Sweet redcurrant butter

100g/4oz unsalted butter, softened

1$\frac{1}{2}$ tablespoons redcurrant jelly

$\frac{1}{2}$ teaspoon salt

freshly ground black pepper

3 tablespoons fresh parsley, finely chopped

1 To make the marinade: Put the chopped shallot, garlic, juniper berries, bay leaf, rosemary, wine and olive oil into a large bowl. Season and mix very well. Lay the steaks in a single layer in a large shallow dish. Pour the marinade over them, cover and leave to marinate in the refrigerator for at least 2 hours.

2 To make the sweet redcurrant butter: Put the softened butter into a large bowl and beat in the redcurrant jelly, salt and black pepper to taste. Spoon the butter onto a large piece of cling film and roll up. Twist the ends like a Christmas cracker to form a neat log shape. Spread the parsley on a large plate. Unwrap the butter and roll in the parsley until coated evenly all over. Wrap in a clean piece of cling film and chill in the refrigerator until firm.

3 Remove the steaks from the marinade and discard the marinade. Lightly season the steaks and barbecue over Direct Medium heat for 6–8 minutes, turning once, until just tender but each steak is still a deep crimson colour in the centre. Cut the butter into 6 slices and serve on top of the hot grilled steaks.

Rack of venison
with garlic & rosemary

main course: serves 6	**gas:** indirect / medium heat	**charcoal:** indirect	**prep time:** 15 mins + marinating	**barbecue time:** 40 mins

A hearty Italian red wine and salty pancetta give this dish a rich flavour. A rack of venison should be prepared much like a rack of lamb. Ask your butcher to French trim the rack, which means removing the back or chine bone, cutting and cleaning between the rib bones and removing most of the fat, leaving just a thin layer.

1.25–1.5kg/2½–3lb rack of venison, French trimmed

3 plump garlic cloves

small bunch of fresh rosemary

25g/1oz piece of fatty pancetta

salt

freshly ground black pepper

1 bottle of full-bodied Italian red wine, preferably Barolo

oil, for brushing

Rosemary and garlic butter, to serve (page 15)

1 Trim any excess fat from the rack of venison. Make small deep incisions all over the meat on the rack. Slice the garlic cloves thinly. Break off small sprigs of rosemary and cut the pancetta into slivers about the size of the garlic slices. Stuff a garlic slice, a rosemary sprig and a piece of pancetta into each incision. Put into a shallow dish, season well and pour the wine over it. Marinate for at least 4 hours in the refrigerator, turning occasionally.

2 Remove the rack from the marinade and discard the marinade. Blot the rack dry with kitchen paper. Wrap each rib bone with foil, to protect it during the cooking. Brush the meat all over with oil and season with salt and pepper.

3 Barbecue, bone side down, over Indirect Medium heat for 35–40 minutes, turning halfway through cooking time. Remove the foil off the bones for the last 5 minutes of the cooking time. Leave to rest for 5 minutes before serving.

4 Cut between the bones and serve the cutlets with slices of the rosemary and garlic butter.

DID YOU KNOW? Garlic only flavours a dish as much as you let it. It is at its mildest in a dish when it is used as a whole and unpeeled clove as no juices are allowed to escape. Peeled whole garlic gives a slightly stronger flavour, while sliced and crushed cloves can become quite pungent and powerful in scent and flavour. So, the more finely you cut or crush it, the more flavour it releases.

Wild boar sausages
with grilled porcini salsa

main course: serves 4	gas: indirect / medium heat	charcoal: indirect	prep time: 10 mins	barbecue time: 32 mins

The most celebrated Italian mushroom is the porcini, which has a deep rich flavour and soft texture. If you find porcini mushrooms are difficult to get hold of, use field or Portobello mushrooms as an alternative – they won't have the same flavour but will still make a satisfying salsa.

Grilled porcini salsa

450g/1lb fresh porcini mushrooms

1 onion, cut into 1.5cm/$^1/_2$ inch slices

oil, for brushing

6 plum tomatoes, skinned, deseeded and chopped

2 tablespoons fresh marjoram, chopped

1 tablespoon balsamic vinegar

2 tablespoons extra virgin olive oil

salt

freshly ground black pepper

8 wild boar sausages

polenta (see page 131), to serve

1 To make the porcini salsa: Brush the mushrooms and onion slices all over with the oil. Barbecue over Direct Medium heat for 10–12 minutes, turning once until tender and just browned. Put aside to cool.

2 Roughly chop the mushrooms and onions and put into a mixing bowl. Add the chopped tomato and marjoram and toss well. Add the vinegar, olive oil and plenty of seasoning and toss again. Put aside until required, but don't chill as this dulls the flavours.

3 Brush the sausages lightly with oil and barbecue over Indirect Medium heat for 15–20 minutes turning once, until tender.

4 Serve the sausages with a spoonful of the grilled porcini salsa and some soft polenta.

Grilled italian sausages on polenta with salsa verde

| main course: serves 4 | gas: direct / medium & high heat | charcoal: direct | prep time: 20 mins + cooling | barbecue time: 26 mins |

Italian pork sausages for cooking (not to be confused with cured sausages) are usually made of pork with herbs and spices, and sometimes red wine. Here they are served with grilled polenta, although you could serve them with soft mashed polenta like a sort of Italian bangers and mash. Serve with a pungent, herby salsa verde.

150g/5oz instant polenta

½ teaspoon salt

25g/1oz Parmesan cheese, grated

2 tablespoons fresh parsley, chopped

3 tablespoons olive oil

8 large, plump Italian pork sausages

oil, for brushing

Salsa verde, to serve (page 23)

1 Bring 750ml/1¼ pints water to the boil. Stir in the polenta and salt and whisk well to prevent any lumps from forming. Bring back to the boil, then lower the heat. Cook gently for 8–10 minutes or according to packet instructions, stirring continuously. Stir in the Parmesan, parsley and oil, and mix thoroughly. Pour into a shallow greased dish so the polenta is about 1.5cm/½ inch thick. Leave to cool and set.

2 Cut the polenta into 8 slices or squares. Brush the sausages lightly with oil and barbecue over Direct Medium heat for 15–18 minutes, turning once. Remove and keep warm.

3 Meanwhile, brush both sides of the polenta slices well with oil. Barbecue over Direct High heat for 8 minutes, turning once, until hot and marked by the cooking grate.

4 Serve the sausages with the grilled polenta pieces and a spoonful of salsa verde on the side.

Did you know? Polenta is the Italian word for a cooked dish made from ground maize, but is sometimes used to describe the uncooked grain too. Polenta is extremely versatile. You can serve it hot, or let it go cold and cook it again. It can also be used in cakes or biscuits instead of flour to provide a texture similar to ground nuts.

Pork & chorizo kebabs on minted broad beans

| main course: serves 4 | gas: direct / medium heat | charcoal: direct | prep time: 40 mins | barbecue time: 10 mins |

In Spain, chorizo sausages are usually fried and served with crusty bread to soak up the juices. In this version, the cubes of granary bread soak up the marinade and the oils seeping from the chorizo while it is barbecuing.

675g/1½lb fresh or frozen broad beans, shelled

10 tablespoons olive oil

150g/5oz Serrano ham, chopped

4 plump garlic cloves, crushed

120ml/4fl oz chicken stock

2 pork tenderloins, each weighing 350–450g/12oz–1lb

2 x 2.5cm/1 inch-thick slices of granary bread

8 thin slices of chorizo sausage, cut in half

¼ teaspoon chilli powder

1 teaspoon fresh sage, chopped

salt

freshly ground black pepper

4 tablespoons fresh mint, chopped

1 If using wooden or bamboo skewers, soak 4 in cold water for at least 30 minutes. Meanwhile, drop the broad beans into a pan of boiling salted water, bring back to the boil and cook the beans for 1–2 minutes. Drain and refresh under cold running water.

2 In a frying pan, heat 4 tablespoons of the oil and add the ham, garlic and drained beans. Add the stock, cover and cook for 20–25 minutes over a low heat, until the beans are very tender.

3 While the beans are cooking, trim the pork tenderloins of any excess fat and silver skin. Cut the meat into 2.5 cm/1 inch cubes, to produce 20 pieces in all. Cut the bread into 20 cubes slightly smaller than the pork cubes.

4 Thread the pork, bread and chorizo on the skewers, so each skewer has 5 pieces of pork, 5 pieces of bread and 4 half slices of chorizo. Mix the remaining 6 tablespoons of oil, with the chilli powder, sage and plenty of seasoning, and brush over the skewers.

5 Barbecue the skewers over Direct Medium heat for 8–10 minutes, turning once and brushing with a little more chilli oil (use a clean basting brush), until cooked through.

6 Stir the mint into the warm broad beans. Spoon the broad beans and ham on to a platter, lay the kebabs on top and serve.

Pork tenderloin flavoured with smoked paprika

main course: serves 6–8	gas: indirect / medium heat	charcoal: direct	prep time: 20 mins + marinating	barbecue time: 35 mins

For this pork dish, look for smoked paprika. Unlike regular paprika, where the peppers are sun-dried, in Spain they are dried over oak fires to impart a distinctive smoky flavour. The most popular brand is *La Chinata*.

6 plump garlic cloves

1 teaspoon salt

4 tablespoons olive oil

2 tablespoons fresh parsley, chopped

1 tablespoon fresh oregano, chopped

1 teaspoon fresh rosemary, chopped

1 teaspoon fresh thyme, chopped

2 dried bay leaves, crushed

$\frac{1}{2}$ teaspoon coarsely ground black pepper

2 tablespoons smoked paprika

3 pork tenderloins, each weighing about 350–450g/ 12oz–1lb

Romesco sauce (page 21), to serve

Country-style potato salad (page 181), to serve

1 The day before, grind the garlic and salt together roughly, using a mortar and pestle. Add the olive oil and continue crushing to an almost smooth paste. Transfer to a medium-sized bowl. Stir in the parsley, oregano, rosemary, thyme, bay leaves, pepper and paprika to make a thick paste.

2 Trim off any excess fat and silver skin from the pork tenderloins. With the tip of a sharp knife, make little slits all over the tenderloins. Rub the garlic and herb paste all over the surface of the tenderloins. Put on a large plate, cover with cling film and put in the refrigerator to marinate overnight. If possible, leave for 24 hours.

3 Before cooking the meat, let it come back to room temperature. Barbecue the tenderloins over Indirect Medium heat for 30–35 minutes, turning once, until cooked through. Leave to rest for 10 minutes before slicing.

4 Slice thickly and serve with a potato salad and a little Romesco sauce on the side.

Balsamic-glazed spareribs with chilli dipping sauce

| **main course:** serves 4 | **gas:** indirect / medium heat | **charcoal:** direct | **prep time:** 15 mins | **barbecue time:** 1 hour 10 mins |

Barbecued pork spareribs are not all that common in Italy, but no barbecue book would be complete without a rib recipe. The famous vinegar of Modena, which makes a delicious glaze when reduced, gave the Italian inspiration to this dish.

300ml/½ pint balsamic vinegar

2 medium red chillies, deseeded and finely chopped

2.75kg/6lb pork spareribs in 2 or 3 slabs

oil, for brushing

salt

freshly ground black pepper

1 Put the balsamic vinegar and chopped chillies into a medium-sized saucepan and bring to the boil. Reduce the heat and simmer for 8–10 minutes, until a thick glaze is achieved. It will thicken a little more as it cools. Put aside.

2 Brush the spareribs all over with oil and season very well. Barbecue the slabs of ribs over Indirect Medium heat for 1 hour–1 hour 10 minutes, turning once during cooking. During the last 10 minutes of cooking time, brush the uppermost side of the ribs with the balsamic glaze (using a clean basting brush).

3 Once the ribs are cooked, leave to cool slightly for a minute or two, then cut into individual ribs and serve.

DID YOU KNOW? There are a huge amount of chilli varieties, ranging from the very hot habañero to the milder jalapeño chilli. Always remember to add chilli to dishes by taste – as each variety varies in heat so much you should only use as much as you can handle.

Pork, lemon & potato kebabs

main course: serves 4	gas: direct / medium heat	charcoal: direct	prep time: 20 mins	barbecue time: 14 mins

These kebabs are simple to make and barbecue. They use the thick woody branches of the rosemary bush as the skewers, which helps to impart flavour into the pork and potatoes. Use regular skewers if you have to, increasing the rosemary to 2 tablespoons in the marinade.

8 fresh rosemary branches, each about 15cm/6 inches long

16 baby new potatoes

675g/1$\frac{1}{2}$lb pork tenderloin

3 tablespoons olive oil

$\frac{1}{2}$ lemon, juice only

salt

freshly ground black pepper

lemon wedges, to serve

1 Pull most of the leaves off the rosemary branches, leaving just a tuft of rosemary at the tip and reserving the leaves. Soak the rosemary branches in cold water for at least 30 minutes. Roughly chop enough of the rosemary leaves to give you about 1 tablespoon (you won't want all the leaves).

2 Cook the potatoes in boiling salted water for 10–12 minutes until barely tender. Drain well.

3 Trim the pork of any excess fat and silver skin and cut it into 4cm/1$\frac{1}{2}$ inch cubes (about 24 cubes in all). Thread the pork cubes alternately with the potatoes onto the rosemary skewers.

4 Mix the chopped rosemary, olive oil and lemon juice together. Season well and put aside.

5 Brush the rosemary and lemon marinade over the pork skewers and season with salt and pepper. Barbecue the skewers over Direct Medium heat for 14 minutes, turning once and brushing again (using a clean basting brush) halfway through the cooking.

6 Serve with lemon wedges.

Figs & mozzarella wrapped in prosciutto

appetiser: serves 6	gas: indirect / medium heat	charcoal: indirect	prep time: 15 mins	barbecue time: 10 mins

This is a deceptively easy appetiser for a smart dinner party. Use the best buffalo mozzarella, which has a softer texture and sweeter flavour than its rubbery, mass-produced counterpart.

150g/5oz buffalo mozzarella, drained

6 fresh figs

6 slices of prosciutto

3 tablespoons extra virgin olive oil

2 tablespoons balsamic vinegar

salt

freshly ground black pepper

oil, for brushing

1 Cut the mozzarella into 6 pieces. Cut each fig in half. Sandwich a piece of mozzarella between 2 fig halves. Sit this on a slice of prosciutto and wrap the ham up around the fig to encase completely. Repeat to make 6 parcels in all.

2 Whisk the olive oil and balsamic vinegar together, season well and put aside.

3 Brush each fig parcel with a little oil and barbecue over Indirect Medium heat for 8–10 minutes, until the ham is crisp and the cheese has begun to melt.

4 Put a wrapped fig in the centre of each plate and drizzle over the balsamic dressing. Serve warm. Alternatively, you could arrange the figs on a serving platter and let guests help themselves. You could also serve this with a rocket and tomato salad.

DID YOU KNOW? True buffalo mozzarella is a soft-ripening cheese that lasts for five to six weeks. It starts out chalky and becomes creamier the longer it sits. Ideally it should be almost spreadable when eaten.

vegetables on the grill

Red pepper, aubergine & coriander dip

appetiser: serves 4–6	gas: direct / medium heat	charcoal: direct	prep time: 20 mins	barbecue time: 25 mins

This dip is good served with pre-dinner drinks or as part of a *meze*, or indeed as an appetiser in its own right. It is also delicious served with barbecued lamb.

2 aubergines

2 red peppers

oil, for brushing

2 plump garlic cloves, crushed

¼ teaspoon ground cumin

¼ teaspoon paprika

½ lemon, juice only

salt

freshly ground black pepper

150ml/¼ pint Greek yoghurt

4 tablespoons fresh coriander, roughly chopped

pitta bread, to serve

1 Lightly brush the whole aubergines and peppers with oil and barbecue over Direct Medium heat for 20–25 minutes, turning once, until they are blackened and very tender. Remove from the barbecue and put the aubergines aside to cool. Put the peppers into a bag, close tightly and leave to cool for 10–15 minutes.

2 When the aubergine is cool enough to handle, scoop out the soft flesh from the skins into a food processor. Take the cool peppers out of the bag and peel off the charred skin. Cut the tops off the peppers, scoop out the seeds and discard. Add the flesh to the food processor. Add the garlic, cumin, paprika, lemon juice and plenty of seasoning. Blend to a purée.

3 Add the yoghurt and coriander, and blend briefly again. Check the seasoning. Warm the pitta bread on the barbecue for 1–2 minute(s) or, if you are finished with your barbecue at this point, warm the pitta bread in a toaster. Cut each pitta into strips and serve with the dip.

DID YOU KNOW? Sweet peppers include both the familiar bell peppers and also the elongated Italian pepper. All bell peppers start out green; some remain like this, whilst others ripen to their characteristic colour and become sweeter in the process.

Chargrilled aubergine
with broad bean purée

appetiser: serves 4	gas: direct / medium heat	charcoal: direct	prep time: 25 mins	barbecue time: 10 mins

Traditionally this purée is made using dried broad beans, which are more common in the hot Mediterranean countries. Here fresh or frozen broad beans are used for the best flavour and colour.

900g/2lb fresh broad beans, shelled or 400g/14oz frozen broad beans

2 tablespoons olive oil

1 plump garlic clove, crushed

2 red chillies, deseeded and finely chopped

1/2 lemon, juice only

salt

freshly ground black pepper

2–3 tablespoons fresh mint, chopped

2 aubergines, cut into 1.5cm/1/2 inch slices

oil, for brushing

fresh crusty bread, to serve

1 Bring a large saucepan of salted water to the boil and cook the broad beans for 2 minutes, until just tender. Drain and refresh under cold running water and drain again. Remove the tough outer skin of the broad beans and discard. Put the broad beans aside.

2 Heat the olive oil in a large pan and cook the garlic and chilli gently for 3–4 minutes until just softened. Add the beans and cook for 1 minute. Transfer to a food processor, add the lemon juice and blend to a smooth purée. Season well and stir in the chopped mint. Put aside.

3 Brush both sides of the aubergine slices with plenty of oil and season well. Barbecue the aubergine slices over Direct Medium heat for 8–10 minutes, turning once, until tender.

4 Remove the aubergine slices and put on a serving dish with the warm purée. Serve fresh crusty bread on the side.

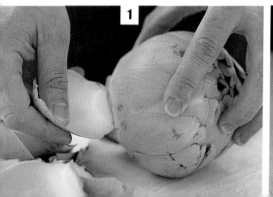

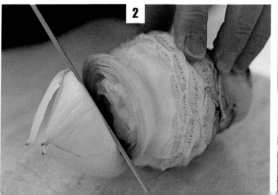

Artichokes with goat cheese & sweet basil dressing

main course: serves 4	gas: direct / medium heat	charcoal: direct	prep time: 45 mins	barbecue time: 12 mins

The warm dressing and goat cheese make the perfect complement to smoky, fresh grilled artichokes, found in most Mediterranean countries. Globe artichokes are best cooked the day you buy them, but if you must keep them a day or two, peel the stem using a potato peeler and put them in a wide dish of water so that just the stems are in the water.

Sweet basil dressing

6 tablespoons extra virgin olive oil

4 garlic cloves, crushed

2 tablespoons white wine vinegar

3 teaspoons sugar

large handful of fresh basil, roughly chopped

salt

freshly ground black pepper

12 medium-sized globe artichokes

oil, for brushing

350g/12oz creamy goat cheese

Italian bean salad (page 179) and crusty bread, to serve

1 To make the dressing: Put the olive oil into a small pan and heat gently. Add the garlic and cook over a very gentle heat for 1–2 minutes, until softened but not browned. Add the white wine vinegar and sugar and stir until the sugar has dissolved. Remove from the heat and put aside. Once the dressing is cool, stir in the chopped basil and season well.

2 Trim the stems of the artichokes, leaving about 1.5cm/^{1}/$_2$ inch of the stem attached. **1** Pull off the tough, darker green leaves until you reach the core of the tender, paler-green leaf. **2** Slice off the top part of the core, then halve lengthwise. **3** Slice away the hairy choke and small purple leaves from the centre and discard. Put the prepared artichokes into a large steamer and place the steamer over a pan of boiling water. Cover and steam for 20–30 minutes until tender, making sure the water doesn't boil dry. Plunge the artichokes into cold water and drain well.

3 Brush the artichokes with oil, and barbecue them over Direct Medium heat for 8–12 minutes, turning once, until slightly charred.

4 Transfer the cooked artichokes to a bowl, pour the basil dressing over them and serve warm, accompanied by the goat cheese, an Italian bean salad and plenty of crusty bread.

Charred artichokes with spiced lemon & honey dressing

main course: serves 4	gas: direct / medium heat	charcoal: direct	prep time: 45 mins	barbecue time: 12 mins

Globe artichokes are great for entertaining as all the preparation work is done in advance and the steamed artichokes can be quickly barbecued at the last moment then served with the cooled dressing. You can also leave the artichokes to marinate in the dressing for a few hours for a more intense flavour, and serve them cold.

12 medium-sized globe artichokes

3 tablespoons extra virgin olive oil

3 garlic cloves, crushed

$^1/_2$ teaspoon ground ginger

pinch of ground turmeric

1 lemon, juice and grated zest

2 tablespoons runny honey

salt

freshly ground black pepper

oil, for brushing

1 Trim the stems of the artichokes, leaving about 1.5cm/$^1/_2$ inch of the stem attached. Pull off the tough darker green leaves until you reach the core of the tender, paler-green leaves. Slice off the top part of the core, then halve lengthwise and slice away the hairy choke and small purple leaves from the centre (see pages 146–147). Put the artichokes into a large steamer and place the steamer over a pan of boiling water. Cover and steam for 20–30 minutes until tender, making sure the water doesn't boil dry. Plunge the artichokes into cold water and drain well. Put aside in a shallow dish.

2 In a large pan, heat the olive oil and add the garlic. Cook gently for 1–2 minute(s), until just softened but not browned. Remove from the heat and stir in the ginger, turmeric, lemon juice and zest, honey and seasoning. Add 150ml/$^1/_4$ pint cold water. Bring to the boil, reduce the heat and simmer for 10–12 minutes, until reduced by half and slightly thickened. Put aside to cool. Season well.

3 Brush the artichokes with oil, and barbecue the artichokes over Direct Medium heat for 8–12 minutes, turning once, until slightly charred. Transfer to a bowl, pour the dressing over them and serve while the artichokes are still warm.

Grilled asparagus with gorgonzola sauce

appetiser: serves 4	gas: direct / medium heat	charcoal: direct	prep time: 15 mins	barbecue time: 8 mins

The gorgonzola sauce is extremely rich, being made with butter and two Italian cheeses, including mascarpone. And, if that's not enough, it is served with a third Italian cheese, Parmesan. However, paired with the grilled asparagus it is a match made in heaven.

Gorgonzola sauce

25g/1oz unsalted butter

200g/7oz Gorgonzola cheese, cut into small pieces

50g/2oz mascarpone cheese

freshly ground black pepper

small handful of basil leaves, torn

24 asparagus spears

oil, for brushing

grated Parmesan, to serve

1 To make the Gorgonzola sauce: Melt the butter in a medium-sized saucepan and add the Gorgonzola. Warm over a very gentle heat until it just becomes liquid. Remove from the heat and stir in the mascarpone, a little black pepper and the basil leaves. Stir until just liquid and remove from the heat.

2 Meanwhile, trim the woody ends from the asparagus spears: Hold a spear at each end with both hands and bend. The spear will snap just where the tough woody end begins. Repeat with all the spears, discarding the woody ends.

3 Brush the spears with oil, and barbecue over Direct Medium heat for 6–8 minutes, turning once, until tender and marked by the grill.

4 Serve the grilled asparagus with the warm sauce and scattered with freshly grated Parmesan.

DID YOU KNOW? Asparagus begins it's life as a tiny black seed. About a year after planting, the seed develops long, tubular roots and is then called a crown. The crowns are transplanted to fields where they are placed in deep trenches and covered with 10 to 12 inches of soil. It then takes two years before the plant is ready to be harvested. The fields are harvested every spring thereafter and will continue to produce for 15 to 20 years.

Charred asparagus spears with garlic, saffron & paprika butter

lunch or appetiser: serves 4	gas: direct / medium heat	charcoal: direct	prep time: 15 mins	barbecue time: 11 mins

In Andalusia, in the early spring, the locals go out to pick the wild asparagus. It is commonly cooked in omelettes or other egg dishes. Here is a barbecue version of a traditional Andalusian asparagus dish.

large pinch of saffron strands

175g/6oz butter, softened

2 plump garlic cloves, crushed

¼ teaspoon paprika

2 tablespoons fresh parsley, chopped

24 asparagus spears

oil, for brushing

4 thick slices of crusty country-style bread

salt

freshly ground black pepper

4 eggs, freshly soft-boiled (about 4–5 minutes), to serve

1 Crush the saffron strands finely using a mortar and pestle and put aside.

2 Melt 50g/2oz of the butter in a small saucepan. Add the garlic and cook gently over a low heat for 1–2 minutes until softened. Stir in the saffron and the paprika, and cook for 1 minute. Stir in the remaining butter and parsley and remove from the heat. Put aside to allow to melt slowly.

3 To trim the woody ends from the asparagus spears, hold a spear at each end with both hands and bend. The spear will snap just where the tough woody end begins. Repeat with all the spears discarding the woody ends.

4 Brush the spears with oil, and barbecue over Direct Medium heat for 6–8 minutes, turning once, until marked by the grill. Barbecue the bread over Direct Medium heat for 2–3 minutes, turning once, until toasted and marked by the grill.

5 Season the flavoured butter and reheat very gently. Put the toasted bread on plates and arrange 6 asparagus spears on top. Drizzle over the flavoured butter. Serve each with a warm, soft-boiled egg.

Grilled vegetables moroccan style

main course: serves 4	gas: direct / medium heat	charcoal: direct	prep time: 40 mins	barbecue time: 12 mins

Based on the classic Moroccan stew 'seven vegetables with couscous', where traditionally the vegetables are stewed with lamb or chicken. Here, the stew is made separately and the barbecued vegetables are served with plain buttered couscous.

1 large aubergine

2 courgettes

1 red pepper

1 yellow pepper

1 small butternut squash

2 red onions

7 tablespoons olive oil

6 plum tomatoes, skinned and roughly chopped

good pinch of saffron strands

$1/2$ teaspoon sugar

3 tablespoons Harissa (page 21)

14oz/400g can of chickpeas, drained and rinsed

3 tablespoons fresh coriander, chopped

3 tablespoons fresh mint, chopped

450ml/$3/4$ pint vegetable stock

salt

freshly ground black pepper

350g/12oz couscous

100g/4oz butter, melted

1 Trim the ends from the aubergine and courgettes. Cut both into 1.5cm/$1/2$ inch thick slices. Half and deseed both peppers. Cut each into 8 wide strips. Peel the butternut squash. Cut in half and scoop out the seeds. Cut each half into slices 1.5cm/$1/2$ inch thick. Cut 1 red onion into 8 wedges. Put all of these into a large bowl and put aside.

2 Chop the remaining onion finely. Heat 3 tablespoons of the olive oil in a large saucepan. Add the chopped onion and cook for 3–4 minutes until softened. Add the chopped tomatoes and saffron, and cook over a low heat for 8–10 minutes. Add the sugar and harissa, and cook for 1 minute. Add the chickpeas, coriander, mint, vegetable stock and seasoning, and cook over a low heat for 10 minutes. Remove from the heat and put aside.

3 Drizzle the remaining 4 tablespoons of olive oil over the vegetables, add some salt and pepper and toss well until the vegetables are coated all over. Barbecue them over Direct Medium heat for 8–12 minutes, turning once, until tender.

4 Meanwhile, tip the couscous into a measuring jug and soak it in an equal amount of hot salted water for 5 minutes, until all the water has been absorbed and the grains are plump and tender. Rub between your fingers to break up any lumps. Transfer to a steamer and steam for 5 minutes.

5 Transfer the couscous to a serving bowl and stir the melted butter through it. Divide between plates, put a ladleful of the hot sauce on the side and serve with the grilled vegetables.

Grilled vegetables in pitta bread
with feta & hummus

main course: serves 4	gas: direct / medium heat	charcoal: direct	prep time: 15 mins + marinating	barbecue time: 13 mins

Pitta bread makes a wonderful natural container for all sorts of grilled vegetables. Grilling the bread directly over the heat not only warms the bread but gives the outside a crisp finish. You can use any vegetables suitable for the barbecue.

2 medium-sized courgettes

1 yellow pepper

1 red pepper

1 large bunch of spring onions

4 tablespoons extra virgin olive oil

2 plump garlic cloves, crushed

1 tablespoon fresh oregano, chopped

1 lemon, juice only

salt

freshly ground black pepper

100g/4oz feta cheese

4 pitta breads, split open

4 tablespoons hummus

1 Trim the ends from the courgettes, and cut at an angle into 1.5cm/$\frac{1}{2}$ inch slices. Halve the peppers and remove the stalks, seeds and white membrane. Cut the flesh into thick strips. Trim the ends from the spring onions and cut into 5cm/2 inch lengths. Whisk the olive oil, garlic, oregano and 2 tablespoons of lemon juice together with plenty of seasoning, and pour over the vegetables. Cover and leave to marinate in a cool place for 2 hours.

2 Barbecue the vegetables over Direct Medium heat for 4–5 minutes. Remove the spring onions from the grill and put into a bowl. Continue barbecuing the courgettes and peppers for a further 2–3 minutes. Remove the courgettes and add to the spring onion. Continue barbecuing the peppers for a further 2 minutes until tender. Add to the spring onion and courgettes.

3 Crumble over the feta and toss well together. Warm the pitta breads on the barbecue for 2–3 minutes, turning once. Split open the pitta, taking care as they may be full of steam.

4 Put a spoonful of hummus in the bottom of the interior of each pitta, top with the grilled vegetables and feta, and serve warm.

Pan bagnat

lunch: serves 6–8	gas: direct / medium heat	charcoal: direct	prep time: 45 mins + marinating	barbecue time: 12 mins

This is a feast of a sandwich from the Provence region of southern France. A hollowed-out rustic loaf of bread is filled with tender charred vegetables from the barbecue. This is a great recipe to make in advance for picnics.

1 medium-sized aubergine

2 medium-sized courgettes

1 large red pepper

1 large yellow pepper

oil, for grilling

salt

freshly ground black pepper

2 garlic cloves, crushed

6 tablespoons extra virgin olive oil

2 tablespoons white wine vinegar

1 large round rustic bread loaf

3 tablespoons Tapenade (page 23)

400g/14oz buffalo mozzarella, sliced

3 tablespoons Pesto (page 20)

bunch of large fresh basil leaves

6 plum tomatoes sliced

1 The day before, trim the ends from the aubergine, and cut it into 1.5cm/$\frac{1}{2}$ inch slices. Trim the ends from the courgettes and cut lengthwise into 1.5cm/$\frac{1}{2}$ inch slices. Halve the peppers and remove the stalks, seeds and white membrane. Cut the flesh of the peppers into wide strips.

2 Toss all the vegetable slices with plenty of oil and seasoning and barbecue over Direct Medium heat for 8–12 minutes, turning once, until tender.

3 Put the cooked vegetables into a large shallow dish. Mix the crushed garlic, olive oil and vinegar together and pour over the barbecued vegetables. Put aside to marinate for 2 hours.

4 Meanwhile, cut the top off the loaf of bread and put the top aside. Using your fingers, remove the soft bread from inside the loaf to leave a case with walls about 1.5cm/$\frac{1}{2}$ inch thick. (Freeze the unwanted soft bread dough to make breadcrumbs in the future.)

5 Using a spoon, spread the tapenade in the base of the hollowed out loaf. Top with the aubergine slices in an even layer. Season well. Top this with the mozzarella slices. Spoon over the pesto. Add a layer of courgettes, followed by a layer of red peppers and season well. Top the peppers with a layer of basil leaves. Next add a layer of yellow peppers and finish with a layer of tomato slices and season again. Replace the lid.

6 Wrap the loaf in cling film and stand a few kitchen weights or unopened cans on top to compress the loaf. Chill like this overnight. When ready to serve, cut into wedges.

Bruschetta with barbecued aubergine caponata

appetiser: serves 4–6	gas: direct / medium heat	charcoal: direct	prep time: 20 mins	barbecue time: 13 mins

The classic Italian chutney-like mixture made here could have been invented especially for the barbecue. Prepare the caponata in advance, then serve it warm at the last moment on grilled bread for the perfect accompaniment to pre-dinner drinks.

1 large aubergine

oil, for brushing

8 tablespoons olive oil

1 small onion, finely chopped

1 celery stalk, finely chopped

4 plum tomatoes, skinned, deseeded and chopped

handful of pitted black olives, roughly chopped

2 tablespoons small capers, drained, rinsed and chopped

1 tablespoon sugar

50ml/2fl oz red wine vinegar

2 tablespoons fresh parsley, chopped

salt

freshly ground black pepper

1 loaf of rustic Italian bread, such as ciabatta, cut into 1.5cm/ ½ inch slices

1 plump garlic clove

fresh basil leaves, to serve

1 Trim the ends from the aubergine. Cut it lengthwise into slices 1.5cm/½ inch thick. Brush the slices well with oil and barbecue over Direct Medium heat for 8–10 minutes, turning once. Remove and put aside to cool.

2 Heat 3 tablespoons of the olive oil in a medium-sized saucepan and cook the onion and celery for 4–5 minutes, until the onion has softened. Add the tomatoes, olives and capers, and cook for 10 minutes. Increase the heat and cook for 2–3 minutes. Add the sugar and stir until dissolved. Stir in the vinegar and reduce for 1–2 minutes to a thick pulpy mixture. Dice the barbecued aubergine and stir into the mixture with the parsley and plenty of seasoning. Put aside.

3 Barbecue the slices of bread over Direct Medium heat for 2–3 minutes, turning once, until toasted and marked with the grill.

4 Rub each slice with a peeled garlic clove, drizzle with a little of the remaining 5 tablespoons of oil and top with the warm caponata and a fresh basil leaf. Serve warm.

Falafel

| main course: serves 6 | gas: direct / medium heat | charcoal: direct | prep time: 2–2½ hours + soaking | barbecue time: 12 mins |

This famous dish hails from Egypt, but is now popular in many countries that border the Mediterranean and Middle East. It is sold in all the street markets and *souks*, and is as popular as hamburgers are in Western countries. Traditionally they are deep-fried, but here they are grilled for a great flavour. A great addition to *al fresco* dining.

250g/9oz dried chickpeas

1 teaspoon ground cumin

1 teaspoon ground coriander

pinch of chilli powder

½ teaspoon baking powder

2 spring onions, roughly chopped

3 garlic cloves, crushed

2–3 tablespoons flat leaf parsley, chopped

1 teaspoon salt, plus more for seasoning

1 egg, lightly beaten

2 tablespoons light tahini (sesame seed paste)

1 tablespoon olive oil

freshly ground black pepper

oil, for brushing

6 pitta breads, split open

handful of salad leaves

4 tomatoes, roughly chopped

Tzatziki (page 22), to serve

1 The day before, soak the chickpeas in plenty of cold water for 24 hours.

2 Next day, drain them very well. Put into a pan, cover with cold water and bring to the boil. Cover and cook for 1½–2 hours, until tender. Drain well.

3 Put the chickpeas into a food processor with the cumin, coriander, chilli and baking powder, spring onions, garlic, parsley, and 1 teaspoon salt, and blend to a coarse paste. Transfer to a bowl and stir in the egg, tahini, olive oil and seasoning, to give a soft but stiff mixture.

4 Divide the mixture into 12. Shape each into a ball, then slightly flatten each ball to give a round cake shape. Put on a large flat plate and chill for 30 minutes.

5 Brush these falafel with plenty of oil and barbecue over Direct Medium heat for 8–10 minutes, turning once. Warm the pitta bread on the barbecue for 1–2 minutes, turning once.

6 Fill the pitta bread with salad leaves, chopped tomatoes and a little seasoning. Top with a spoonful of tzatziki. Pop 2 falafel into each pitta and serve warm.

Saganaki

main course: serves 4	gas: direct / low & medium heat	charcoal: direct	prep time: 15 mins + chilling	barbecue time: 11 mins

Traditional saganaki is Greek cheese fried in hot oil with ouzo or brandy and served very hot, straight out of the pan, with fresh lemon juice squeezed on top. In fact, the saganaki is the small two-handled pan in which the Kefalotyri or Kasseri cheese is melted. Here the cheese is wrapped in vine leaves and melted on the barbecue.

1 plump garlic clove, crushed

1 small lemon, grated zest only

16 vine leaves, fresh or in brine

450g/1lb Kefalotyri or Kasseri cheese

salt

freshly ground black pepper

oil, for brushing

4 thick slices of crusty country-style bread

Greek salad (page 182), to serve

1 Mix the garlic clove and grated lemon zest together. Put aside.

2 If using fresh vine leaves, drop them into a pan of boiling water for a few seconds until they just flop and loose their stiffness. If using leaves in brine, soak them briefly in hot water to remove the salt. Drain and wash the prepared vine leaves under cold running water, then pat dry. Cut out the tough stem. Cut the cheese into 50g/2oz pieces, about 1.5cm/^{1}/$_2$ inch thick. Put 2 leaves on the work surface, slightly overlapping. Place a piece of cheese in the centre. Sprinkle over a little of the garlic and lemon zest mixture, and check the seasoning. Wrap the leaves around the cheese and place, seam side down, on a large plate. Repeat with the remaining cheese, leaves and garlic and lemon zest. Chill for 2 hours.

3 Brush the vine-wrapped cheese packets with oil and barbecue over Direct Low heat for 4–5 minutes turning once halfway through, until the leaves are slightly charred. Remove.

4 Barbecue the bread over Direct Medium heat for 1–1^1/$_2$ minutes on each side, turning once until toasted and marked with the grill.

5 Serve the saganaki with a fresh Greek salad, omitting the feta if you like.

Grilled halloumi & courgettes
with roasted pepper purée

| **main course:** serves 4 | **gas:** direct / medium heat | **charcoal:** direct | **prep time:** 20 mins + cooling | **barbecue time:** 28 mins |

Halloumi is one of the cheeses best suited to barbecuing because of its good cooking qualities. It is often grilled and served hot as part of a Greek *meze*. The smokiness of the red pepper sauce enlivens the mild flavours of the halloumi and courgettes.

Red pepper and feta purée

2 red peppers

2 red onions, cut into 1.5cm/ 1/2 inch slices

oil, for brushing

200g/7oz feta cheese

1–2 tablespoons red wine vinegar

1 teaspoon fresh thyme leaves

Lemon dressing

6 tablespoons extra virgin olive oil

1 small lemon, juice only

2 teaspoons fresh oregano, chopped

salt

freshly ground black pepper

4 medium-sized courgettes

225g/8oz halloumi cheese, thickly sliced

crusty bread, to serve

1 To make the red pepper and feta purée: Brush the peppers and onion slices with oil, and barbecue over Direct Medium heat for 12–15 minutes, turning 2–3 times during cooking, until tender. Remove from the heat, put the peppers into a bag and close tightly. Set aside until cool enough to handle. Put the onion aside to cool.

2 Once the peppers are cool enough, remove them from the bag and peel away the charred skin. Cut off the tops and remove the seeds from the peppers, then chop the flesh. Chop the onion finely. Put both into a food processor with the feta cheese, vinegar and thyme, and blend to a purée. Put aside.

3 To make the lemon dressing: Whisk the olive oil, 2 tablespoons of lemon juice, oregano and seasoning together, and put aside.

4 Trim the ends from the courgettes and cut lengthways into 1.5cm/1/2 inch slices. Brush with oil and barbecue over Direct Medium heat for 6–8 minutes, turning halfway through, until tender and marked with the grill. Remove from the grill and put on to a warm platter.

5 Brush the halloumi slices with oil and barbecue for 4–5 minutes, turning once. When they are marked with the grill and just soft, remove and add to the platter.

6 Drizzle the courgettes and cheese with the lemon dressing and serve warm with the red pepper and feta purée, and plenty of crusty bread.

Roasted peppers stuffed with rice & butter beans

main course: serves 6	gas: direct / medium heat	charcoal: direct	prep time: 45 mins	barbecue time: 15 mins

Ramiros peppers are long sweet peppers that can be red or yellow. Because they vary in size, you may have some stuffing left over; if you do, wrap the remaining stuffing in foil and place it on the cooking grate. Heat through for 5–8 minutes until piping hot and serve with the peppers.

Stuffing

2 tablespoons olive oil

1 onion, finely chopped

2 plump garlic cloves, crushed

2 teaspoons sweet paprika

225g/8oz long-grain rice

200g/7oz can of chopped tomatoes

450ml/ ¾ pint vegetable stock

200g/7oz can of butter beans, drained and rinsed

75g/3oz frozen peas

2 tablespoons fresh parsley, chopped

salt

freshly ground black pepper

6 red or yellow Ramiros peppers

100g/4oz Manchego cheese, cut into small dice

1 To make the stuffing: Heat the oil in a large saucepan. Add the onion and garlic, and cook for 3–4 minutes until softened. Add the paprika and cook for 1 minute. Add the rice and stir until well coated with the onion and paprika. Add the chopped tomatoes, the stock, the butter beans and peas. Bring to the boil, cover and cook over a low heat for 10 minutes until just tender. Add the chopped parsley, season well and stir through gently with a fork. Leave to cool.

2 Cut the tops off the peppers and reserve. Shake out the seeds from the peppers. Using a thin-bladed long knife, cut out and discard the white pith or core from each pepper and then season the inside of the peppers with a little salt and pepper.

3 Stir the cheese into the cooled stuffing. Spoon and pack the stuffing into the peppers, pushing it right down into each pepper. Replace the tops on the peppers and secure, using 3–4 cocktail sticks each.

4 Lay the peppers lengthwise on the cooking grate and barbecue over Direct Medium heat for 12–15 minutes, turning twice, until tender.

Portobello mushrooms with porcini & blue cheese filling

main course: serves 6	gas: direct / medium heat	charcoal: direct	prep time: 30 mins + soaking	barbecue time: 13 mins

Impressive in size and appearance, the Portobello mushroom makes an ideal vessel in which to hold a delicious combination of porcini mushrooms and polenta. Dried porcini are widely available now and make a good store-cupboard standby. They are quite pungent, which is why very few need to be used.

15g/^{1}/$_2$oz dried porcini mushrooms

150g/5oz instant polenta

25g/1oz Parmesan cheese

2 tablespoons fresh parsley, chopped

3 tablespoons olive oil

salt

freshly ground black pepper

6 very large field or portobello mushrooms, measuring 12.5cm/5 inches across

oil, for brushing

75g/3oz blue cheese, crumbled

fresh chives, to garnish

1 Soak the porcini mushrooms in 300ml/^{1}/$_2$ pint of boiling water for 30 minutes.

2 Drain well into a measuring jug, reserving the mushrooms. Add enough water to the soaking liquid to make up 750ml/1^1/$_4$ pints. Bring the liquid to the boil. Stir in the polenta and whisk well to prevent any lumps forming. Bring back to the boil then lower the heat. Cook for 10 minutes or according to packet instructions, stirring continuously. Roughly chop the mushrooms and stir into the polenta with the Parmesan, parsley, olive oil and plenty of seasoning. Mix thoroughly.

3 Remove the stalks from the field or portobello mushrooms and discard. Season the mushrooms lightly. Spoon in the polenta to fill each mushroom, and brush the edges with a little olive oil.

4 Barbecue the mushrooms over Direct Medium heat for 8–10 minutes, until tender when pierced with the tip of a knife.

5 Remove from the barbecue and top each mushroom with the blue cheese. Return to the barbecue and continue barbecuing for a further 3 minutes or until the cheese has just melted. Garnish with fresh chives.

Portobello mushrooms with camembert, garlic & basil filling

main course: serves 6	gas: direct / medium heat	charcoal: direct	prep time: 25 mins	barbecue time: 10 mins

The filling for these delicious mushrooms is a sort of poor man's pesto, made with garlic, basil, oil and breadcrumbs, which works fantastically with the meaty mushrooms and the creamy Camembert. Make sure your mushrooms have a good cup shape to hold all the ingredients.

2 plump garlic cloves, crushed

25g/1oz fresh basil leaves

4 tablespoons extra virgin olive oil

65g/2½oz fresh white breadcrumbs

salt

freshly ground black pepper

6 very large field or portobello mushrooms (measuring 12.5cm/5 inches across)

1 beef tomato

200g/7oz Camembert cheese

oil, for brushing

Rocket and Parmesan salad (page 177), to serve

1 Put the crushed garlic and basil into a food processor and process to a paste (if you need to, add a splash of the oil to get it moving in the processor). Add the remaining oil and blend very well. Add 50g/2oz of the breadcrumbs, season and mix well. Put aside.

2 Remove the stalks from the mushrooms and discard. Cut the beef tomato into 6 slices. Put a slice of tomato into each mushroom and season lightly. Divide the basil and garlic breadcrumb mixture between each. Cut the Camembert into slices to fit into the mushrooms. Arrange over the basil and garlic breadcrumb mixture. Sprinkle with the remaining 15g/½oz of breadcrumbs.

3 Barbecue the mushrooms over Direct Medium heat for 8–10 minutes, until tender when pierced with tip of a knife.

4 Serve with a rocket and Parmesan salad.

Spinach & pesto pizza
with two cheeses

main course: serves 4	**gas:** direct / medium heat	**charcoal:** direct	**prep time:** 40 mins + resting	**barbecue time:** 10 mins

Making your own fresh pesto is one of the secrets to this great tasting pizza. If you want to cut corners, check out your local deli counter for freshly made pesto. You can also use a packet of pizza base mix but, really, when in Rome...

2 teaspoons easy-blend dried yeast

1 teaspoon sugar

350g/12oz plain flour

1 teaspoon salt

1½ tablespoons olive oil

Topping

100g/4oz baby spinach leaves

1 quantity Pesto (page 20)

salt

freshly ground black pepper

extra virgin olive oil

250g/9oz cherry tomatoes, halved

handful of black olives

225g/8oz buffalo mozzarella, drained

50g/2oz Parmesan, freshly grated

1 In a large bowl, mix the yeast, sugar, flour and salt. Make a well in the centre and add 200ml/7fl oz of warm water and olive oil. Mix well to make a dough. Knead the dough lightly on a floured surface until smooth. Put into a clean bowl, cover and leave to rise in a warm place until doubled in size.

2 Meanwhile, to make the topping: Put the spinach leaves into a saucepan with just the water that clings to them from washing. Cook for 2–3 minutes until just wilted. Drain well and then squeeze very well to get rid of all the water. Chop roughly and put into a bowl. Stir in the pesto and season.

3 Knead the dough once more for a few minutes. Divide in 2 and roll out each to a pizza base about 25.5cm/10 inches in diameter. Brush one side of each base with olive oil. Slide the bases onto 2 large baking trays, then slide the bases, oiled side down, onto the cooking grate and cook over Direct Medium heat for 2–3 minutes until grill marks are visible. Slide back onto the baking sheet and turn over so the grilled side is facing up.

4 Spread the spinach and pesto mixture over each base. Scatter each with the cherry tomatoes and olives. Tear the mozzarella into pieces and scatter on top. Then scatter with the grated Parmesan.

5 Carefully slide the pizzas back on to the cooking grate and cook for 6–7 minutes, until the cheese has melted.

salads on the side

Panzanella (Italian bread salad)

| side dish: serves 6 | gas: direct / medium heat | charcoal: direct | prep time: 35 mins | barbecue time: 18 mins |

3 yellow peppers

oil, for brushing

2 loaves of stale ciabatta or focaccia bread, thickly sliced

900g/2lb ripe plum tomatoes, skinned

1 red onion, finely chopped

75g/3oz capers, drained and rinsed

150g/5oz pitted black olives

3 plump garlic cloves, crushed

6 tablespoons extra virgin olive oil

1 tablespoon red wine vinegar

salt

freshly ground black pepper

2 handfuls of basil leaves, to garnish

1 Brush the peppers with oil and barbecue them over Direct Medium heat for 12–15 minutes, turning 2–3 times during cooking, until tender and blackened. Remove from the heat, put into a bag and close tightly. Leave for 10–15 minutes to steam off the skins. Barbecue the slices of bread over Direct Medium heat for 2–3 minutes, turning once until toasted and marked with the grill.

2 Remove the peppers from the bag and peel away the charred skins. Cut the tops off the peppers and remove and discard the seeds. Cut the flesh into small pieces. Put into a large bowl.

3 Halve the skinned tomatoes and using a spoon, scoop out the seeds into a sieve set over a bowl to catch the juices. Lightly press the seeds into the sieve to extract as much juice as possible. Put aside. Chop the tomato flesh and add to the peppers together with the onion, capers and olives.

4 Break the barbecued bread into pieces and put into a large clean bowl. Stir the garlic, olive oil, red wine vinegar and plenty of seasoning into the tomato juice and pour over the bread. Toss together well until the bread has absorbed all the juice.

5 On a large platter or serving bowl, make layers of the soaked bread, pepper and tomato mixture and the basil leaves, finishing with a layer of the tomato and pepper mixture. Garnish with a scattering of basil leaves.

Aubergine & tomato pilaf

| side dish: serves 4–6 | gas: direct / medium heat | charcoal: direct | prep time: 30 mins | barbecue time: 10 mins |

4 tablespoons olive oil

1 large onion, chopped

450g/1lb bulgar wheat

5 plum tomatoes, skinned and chopped

2 teaspoons sun-dried tomato paste

2 teaspoons sugar

1 teaspoon ground allspice

$^{1}\!/_{4}$ teaspoon salt, plus more for seasoning

2 medium aubergines

oil, for brushing

freshly ground black pepper

6 tablespoons fresh coriander, roughly chopped

1 Heat the oil in a large saucepan and cook the onion for 3–4 minutes until softened but not browned. Add the bulgar wheat and stir well. Add the tomatoes, tomato paste, sugar, allspice, 350ml/12fl oz water and $^{1}\!/_{4}$ teaspoon of salt. Stir and cook, covered, over a low heat for 15 minutes, adding a little more water if necessary. Remove from the heat, cover and leave to rest for 10 minutes, until the grains are plump and tender.

2 Trim the ends from the aubergines and cut lengthways into 1.5cm/$^{1}\!/_{2}$ inch slices. Brush both sides of the aubergine slices with plenty of oil and season well. Barbecue the aubergine slices over Direct Medium heat for 8–10 minutes, turning once, until tender.

3 Dice the slices and stir into the bulgar wheat with the fresh coriander.

Broad bean, pea & mint couscous

| side dish: serves 4–6 | prep time: 20 mins | cook time: 5 mins |

225g/8oz couscous

3 tablespoons extra virgin olive oil

225g/8oz fresh or frozen peas

225g/8oz fresh or frozen broad beans

4 tomatoes, deseeded and finely chopped

4 tablespoons fresh mint, chopped

salt

freshly ground black pepper

1 Put the couscous into a large bowl and gradually add 250ml/8fl oz of hot water until it is all absorbed. Leave for 5 minutes, until the grains are tender and plump. Add 1 tablespoon of olive oil and rub the grains between your fingers to break up any lumps.

2 Drop the peas and broad beans into boiling salted water and bring back to the boil and cook for 1 minute, until just tender. Drain and refresh under cold running water. Leave to drain well. Remove the tough outer white skins from the broad beans. Stir the peas and beans into the couscous.

3 Stir in the chopped tomatoes and mint. Season the remaining 2 tablespoons of olive oil with salt and pour over the couscous. Use a fork to distribute it through the couscous.

Rocket & parmesan salad

| side dish: serves 4–6 | prep time: 10 mins |

100g/4oz rocket leaves

50g/2oz baby spinach leaves

6 tablespoons extra virgin olive oil

1 lemon, juice only

salt

freshly ground black pepper

75g/3oz Parmesan cheese

1 If using bags of ready-prepared salad leaves, just tip the rocket and spinach leaves into a large serving bowl. If using freshly picked leaves, wash well and dry very well before putting into the bowl.

2 Whisk the olive oil and 2 tablespoons of the lemon juice together with plenty of seasoning.

3 Peel or grate the Parmesan into thin shavings.

4 Just before serving, toss the salad leaves, dressing and Parmesan shavings together.

Fresh grated beetroot salad

side dish: serves 4–6 | **prep time:** 15 mins

Dressing

2 small garlic cloves, crushed

1 tablespoon Dijon mustard

1 tablespoon red wine vinegar

3 tablespoons extra virgin olive oil

salt

freshly ground black pepper

450g/1lb raw baby beetroots

100g/4oz red cabbage, shredded

small bunch of spring onions, shredded

2 tablespoons fresh parsley, chopped

1 To make the dressing: Put the garlic, mustard and vinegar into a bowl and whisk well. Gradually whisk in the olive oil and season well with salt and freshly ground black pepper. Put aside.

2 Peel the beetroots and grate, using a grater or a food processor. Alternatively, if you have one, finely shred the beetroots on a mandolin. Put into a bowl with the shredded cabbage, spring onions and parsley.

3 Drizzle the dressing over the salad and toss together lightly using two forks.

Roquefort & chicory salad

side dish: serves 4 | **prep time:** 15 mins

50g/2oz Roquefort cheese, crumbled

2 tablespoons crème fraîche

1 lemon, juice only

salt

freshly ground black pepper

2 heads of chicory

150g/5oz lamb's lettuce or watercress, or a mixture of the two

50g/2oz walnut pieces

1 Put about a quarter of the cheese into a bowl and beat until softened. Whisk in the crème fraîche and the lemon juice with plenty of seasoning. Put aside.

2 Separate the chicory into leaves, wash and pat dry. Cut each leaf in half lengthwise and put into a bowl. Carefully wash the lamb's lettuce and/or watercress (making sure there's no dirt left), pat dry and add to the chicory leaves.

3 Just before serving, drizzle over the creamy dressing and sprinkle with the remaining Roquefort cheese and the walnuts.

Italian bean salad

side dish: serves 4–6 | **prep time:** 15 mins | **cook time:** 14 mins

7 tablespoons olive oil

1 small onion, finely chopped

2 plump garlic cloves, crushed

1 celery stalk, finely chopped

1 red chilli, deseeded and finely chopped

2 teaspoons fresh oregano, chopped

400g/14oz can each of cannellini beans, borlotti beans and butter beans, drained and rinsed

6 vine-ripened tomatoes, skinned

3 tablespoons fresh parsley, chopped

1 lemon, juice only

salt

freshly ground black pepper

1 Heat 3 tablespoons of the olive oil in a large saucepan and cook the onion, garlic, celery and chilli gently over a low heat for 6–8 minutes until softened.

2 Stir in the oregano and all the drained and rinsed beans, and heat gently for 5–6 minutes, stirring occasionally. Remove from the heat and put aside to cool. Meanwhile, deseed and chop the tomatoes.

3 Stir the chopped tomatoes and parsley into the cooled mixture.

4 Whisk the remaining 4 tablespoons of olive oil with 2 tablespoons of lemon juice and season well with salt and freshly ground black pepper. Just before serving, pour over the bean mixture and toss well.

Artichoke & prosciutto salad

side dish: serves 4 | **prep time:** 15 mins

3 tablespoons extra virgin olive oil

1 lemon, juice only

salt

freshly ground black pepper

4 medium-large fresh globe artichokes

100g/4oz prosciutto or Parma ham, thinly sliced

50g/2oz Parmesan cheese

large handful of wild rocket leaves

1 First, make the dressing (so you can pour it over the artichokes as soon as they are prepared): Put the olive oil, 2 tablespoons of lemon juice and plenty of seasoning into a large bowl and whisk well. Put aside.

2 To prepare the artichokes, break off the stems and discard. Cut off the top half of each 'globe'. Bend back the green leaves, letting them snap off close to the base, until you reach the hairy choke. Slice this away with a small sharp knife, close to the heart. Trim off the dark green base of the leaves. Alternatively, you may find it easier to scrape out with a small spoon (see pages 146–147). Very thinly slice the artichoke hearts, using a mandolin or very sharp knife. Immediately toss the slices with the dressing to avoid discoloration.

3 Lay the slices of prosciutto over the base of a large serving platter and spoon the dressed artichoke salad on top. Thinly shave over the Parmesan, scatter over the rocket leaves and serve.

Country-style potato salad

side dish: serves 6 | **prep time:** 15 mins + cooling | **cook time:** 15 mins

550g/1¼lb waxy new potatoes, such as Pink Fir Apple

½ lemon, juice only

4 tablespoons extra virgin olive oil

2 tablespoons fresh basil, chopped

salt

freshly ground black pepper

1 small red onion, finely chopped

12 pitted green olives, halved

4 plum tomatoes, deseeded and roughly chopped

25g/1oz pine nuts, lightly toasted

4 eggs, hard-boiled and shelled

1 Cook the potatoes in boiling salted water for 12–15 minutes until just tender. Drain well and cut in half lengthways. Put into a large bowl.

2 In a small bowl, whisk together 1 tablespoon of lemon juice, the olive oil, basil and plenty of seasoning. Pour over the potatoes and put aside to cool.

3 Add the chopped onion, olives, chopped tomatoes and pine nuts, and toss well. Just before serving, roughly chop the boiled eggs, scatter over the salad and toss the salad once more.

Greek salad

side dish: serves 4 | **prep time:** 20 mins

6 plum tomatoes

1 cucumber

1 large onion

24 Greek black olives

1 lemon, juice only

6 tablespoons extra virgin olive oil

1 garlic clove, crushed

2 tablespoons fresh oregano, chopped

salt

freshly ground black pepper

225g/8oz feta cheese

1 cos lettuce, to serve

1 Cut the tomatoes into chunks and put in a large bowl. Cut the cucumber lengthwise, scrape out the seeds from the centre with a small spoon and discard. Dice the flesh of the cucumber and add to the tomatoes. Thinly slice the onion and add to the bowl with the olives.

2 In a small bowl put 2 tablespoons of lemon juice, the olive oil, garlic, oregano and plenty of seasoning, and whisk well.

3 Pour this dressing over the tomato and cucumber mixture and toss well. Dice the feta and scatter over the top.

4 Serve the salad with large cos lettuce leaves as a base to the salad.

Orange & watercress salad

side dish: serves 4–6 | **prep time:** 15 mins

4 oranges, preferably navel or Valencia

6 spring onions

175g/6oz fresh watercress

6 tablespoons extra virgin olive oil

salt

freshly ground black pepper

1 Using a small sharp knife, cut the top and bottom off each orange. Stand the orange on a chopping board and cutting from top to bottom, carefully slice away all the skin and white pith. Hold the orange in one hand over a bowl and cut out each segment from between the membranes, letting the segments and juice fall into the bowl. Squeeze out the empty membrane. Strain off and reserve the juice. Put the segments into a serving bowl.

2 Trim the spring onions and finely shred lengthwise into long narrow strands. Add to the orange segments with the watercress.

3 Take 2 tablespoons of the strained orange juice and whisk the olive oil into it with plenty of seasoning. Drizzle over the salad, toss everything together and serve immediately.

Spanish rice salad

| side dish: serves 8 | gas: direct / medium heat | charcoal: direct | prep time: 20 mins | barbecue time: 15 mins |

large pinch of saffron strands

2 medium-sized red peppers

oil, for brushing

250g/9oz basmati rice

1 lemon, grated zest only

1 plump garlic clove

salt

1 teaspoon Dijon mustard

1 tablespoon sherry vinegar

6 tablespoons extra virgin olive oil

200g/7oz frozen peas

250g/9oz cherry tomatoes, halved

400g/14oz can of chickpeas, drained and rinsed

12 pitted black olives, halved

25g/1oz flaked almonds, toasted

3 tablespoons fresh parsley, chopped

1 Put the saffron to soak in 2 tablespoons of hot water.

2 Brush the peppers with oil and barbecue them over Direct Medium heat. Grill until evenly charred on all sides, for about 10–12 minutes, turning once every 3–5 minutes. Remove from the heat and place in a bag. Close tightly and leave for 10–15 minutes to steam off the charred skins.

3 When cool enough to handle, remove the peppers from the bag and peel away the charred skins. Cut the tops off the peppers and remove and discard the seeds. Cut the flesh into strips and put aside.

4 While the peppers are cooking and cooling, bring a large saucepan of salted water to the boil. Add the rice, saffron with its soaking water and the lemon zest. Cover and cook for 10–12 minutes until just tender. Drain well and set aside.

5 Using a mortar and pestle, crush the garlic clove with a good pinch of salt, then transfer to a small bowl. Stir in the mustard and vinegar. Whisk in the olive oil and pour over the warm rice. Leave until cold.

6 Cook the peas for 2–3 minutes in boiling salted water, then refresh under cold running water. Add to the cold rice with the pepper strips, tomato halves, chickpeas, olives, flaked almonds and parsley. Toss well.

barbecue basics

Charcoal barbecuing

The secret of cooking on a charcoal kettle lies in the proper use of the lid and the vent system. Cold air is drawn through the bottom vents to provide the oxygen to the burning coals. The air heats and rises, reflecting off the lid so it circulates around the food and eventually passes out through the top vent. Thus, a kettle barbecue works much like a convection oven, making it ideal not only for sausages and kebabs, but also for larger cuts of meat, such as joints and whole birds.

The art of charcoal barbecuing lies in mastering the fire – knowing how to set it up correctly and then how to control the heat. Part of the challenge of cooking on a charcoal barbecue is learning how to control the temperature. Once you master that, it's easy and fun to cook entire menus and experiment with different combinations – and when you get the timing right, your guests will be able to enjoy all the food hot from the barbecue at the right time!

Building the fire

The two keys to success when building the fire are:

• Use the right fuel – solid hardwood charcoal briquettes are best. Look for either the square or round (also known as beads) types. Stay away from cheaper briquettes or lump wood charcoal, as these contain fillers and do not burn as hot or as long.

• Use fire lighters – the waxy-looking sticks or cubes – whenever possible, as they do not impart the chemical flavour often found when using lighter fluids. Fire lighters also burn in all types of weather, ensuring a fast start to the fire. (If using lighter fluid, use it only on dry coals – never spray it on a lit fire!)

For the best results, follow these instructions:

1 Create a pyramid with the coals in the centre of the charcoal grate. Push three fire lighters into the pyramid and light them, letting the coals catch. Leave the lid off while the coals come up to heat. You can tell the coals are ready when they are covered in a light grey ash, which usually takes about 25–30 minutes (see figure 1 below).

2 Then, use tongs to arrange the coals according to the cooking method called for in the recipe.
1 For Direct cooking (see page 192), you should have an even layer of hot coals across the charcoal grate.
2 For Indirect cooking (see page 193), you should have enough coals (see chart on page 189) to arrange them evenly on either side of the charcoal grate. Use a drip pan between the coals for Indirect cooking.

Placing the coals directly above the vent(s) helps get maximum oxygen to feed the fire. Make sure you have enough spare coals to add each hour for longer roasting times.

A tip about vents – keep them open! The wider the vent opening, the hotter the fire. Place the lid so that the top vent is positioned for maximum air draw and keep this open at all times.

Extinguishing the fire

1 Before you extinguish the coals, remove all food from the cooking grate and replace the lid. Allow the barbecue to continue heating the cooking grate until any smoking stops, 10 to 15 minutes, to burn off any cooking residues. Then give the grate a good brushing with a brass grill brush.

2 Close the lid and all the vents and let the barbecue cool down.

3 Do not handle hot ashes. Wait until they are cold, and remove them so they don't attract moisture and encourage rust. Some grills are equipped with blades that sweep the ashes into ash pans or catchers. Dispose of the ashes properly in a fireproof container. Always remove the ashes before storing a charcoal barbecue.

How much fuel is right?

Use the following charts for your initial settings, depending on the size of your barbecue. The best way to control the temperature of the barbecue is to adjust the number of coals. To get a hotter fire, simply add more coals to your initial settings. For a lower temperature, simply use fewer coals. This may require a little experimentation on your part, but eventually you will know what's right for your barbecue and the foods that you cook most often.

How many briquettes you need to use

BBQ kettle	square traditional briquettes	round charcoal beads
37cm (14$\frac{1}{2}$ inch) diameter	15 each side	12–24 each side
47cm (18$\frac{1}{2}$ inch) diameter	20 each side	28–56 each side
57cm (22$\frac{1}{2}$ inch) diameter	25 each side	44–88 each side
95cm (37$\frac{1}{2}$ inch) diameter	75 each side	4–8kg each side
Charcoal Go-Anywhere®	15 each side	12–24 each side

How many briquettes you need to add per hour for indirect cooking

BBQ kettle	number of coals per side / per hour
37cm (14$\frac{1}{2}$ inch) diameter	6
47cm (18$\frac{1}{2}$ inch) diameter	7
57cm (22$\frac{1}{2}$ inch) diameter	8
95cm (37$\frac{1}{2}$ inch) diameter	22
Charcoal Go-Anywhere®	6

CHIMNEY STARTERS – a well-kept secret
A chimney starter is a metal canister with a handle and an elevated floor that is wonderful for getting the coals started quickly, easily and without fuss. Simply fill the canister with the required number of briquettes, place it over wadded-up newspaper or two fire lighters, light the starter and let the coals catch. You can do all this on the charcoal grate of your barbecue, which protects the canister from wind and provides a draw to help the coals light.

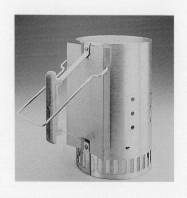

Gas barbecuing

Gas barbecues have one main advantage over charcoal barbecues and that's speed. Once your gas bottle is attached, it's as simple as turning on the oven in your kitchen. Simply push the ignition switch, light the burners and within 10 to 15 minutes the barbecue should be up to heat.

The basic underpinnings of a gas barbecue are simple. First come burners to create heat, then some type of system above the burners to help disburse the heat, such as metal bars, lava rocks, ceramic briquettes, etc. Above this you'll find the cooking grate and underneath the cooking box there will be a system for disposing of debris and fats that have fallen during cooking.

The heart and soul of a gas barbecue are the burners. Not only do they do the job of conducting the fire, but they also put the control of outdoor cooking in your hands. What defines a quality gas barbecue is the ability to adjust and orchestrate the heat settings. This is why you want a gas barbecue with at least three burners; four- to six-burner models are becoming more and more popular. More burners equal more options – and better control. With multiple burners you can set up heat zones, just like on a charcoal barbecue, and use them to cook several foods simultaneously, or the same dish using both Direct and Indirect methods. So while the chicken is roasting, you can barbecue some tender veggies directly over the heat and voilà! Everything is ready at the same time.

Starting the fire

1 Check that there is enough fuel in your gas bottle (some barbecues even have gauges that tell you how much is left). Check to see that all the burner control knobs are turned off.

2 Open the lid. Open the gas valve at the source or turn the valve on the bottle to 'on'.

3 Turn on the starter burner by pushing the ignition switch or lighting a match.

4 Always read the instruction manual for details on your specific model. When the first burner is ignited, light the rest of the burners and switch all of them to High. Close the lid and preheat the barbecue to about 500–550°F/245–275°C. This takes about 10 minutes.

5 Using a brass-bristle brush, clean the grate to eliminate any debris left over from your last cookout.

6 Then, adjust the burner controls according to the cooking method called for in the recipe.

To cook food using the Direct method (see page 192), all three gas burners should be lit.

Turning the fire off

1 Before turning the barbecue off, remove all food from the cooking grate and turn all burners back on to High to let the barbecue come back up to heat. Then use a brass-bristle brush to clean the grates of food and debris.

2 Make sure all burners are switched to 'off'. Then, shut the gas down at the source.

3 When the barbecue has cooled down, preferably the next day, remove the catch pan from the bottom tray, or empty the drip tray so you don't get flare-ups or grease fires the next time you barbecue.

NOTE: Remember, never store your barbecue indoors with the bottle attached. If properly covered, a gas barbecue can withstand the elements outside and always be ready for action.

How do you get the right temperature?

Most gas barbecues today have burner controls that are set to Low, Medium and High, but each model uses a different temperature, so be sure to learn what those are on your model.

The recipes in this book are gauged to temperatures of about 300°F/150°C for Low; 350°F/180°C for Medium; and 500–550°F/245–275°C for High. Some gas barbecues have a built-in thermometer that will tell you the internal temperature, but if yours does not, use an oven thermometer placed on the cooking grate.

SMOKING It's easy to add a more distinctive flavour to barbecued food by adding manufactured or natural flavourings to the smouldering coals, or the smoker box in the case of gas barbecues, before cooking.

There are many types of flavoured woods and herbs available on the market today, such as apple, cherry, maple, hickory, oak and pecan. They come in either chunks or chips, and should be soaked in cold water for at least 30 minutes prior to use. You can also use walnut, hazelnut or almond shells in the same way as wood chips. Natural herbs include woody stalks of rosemary, bay or thyme, and even grape vines. Again, soak in cold water for at least 30 minutes before using.

On a charcoal barbecue: Simply place the soaked chunks, chips or herbs directly on the hot coals. Place the food on the cooking grate and barbecue according to the recipe, allowing the smoke to infuse the food with extra flavour.

On a gas barbecue: If your barbecue has a smoker box accessory, simply follow the manufacturer's instructions – some smoker boxes are 'dry', some others require the addition of a small pan of water for best results. If your barbecue does not have a smoker box accessory, simply place the chunks, chips or herbs in a small metal foil pan, poke holes in the bottom with a skewer and place on top of the heat disbursement system or the cooking grate in one corner. Turn the grill on and, as it heats up, smoke will begin to form, and will continue to flavour the food as it cooks. Never place the food directly over the pan of smoking materials.

A smoker box accessory makes adding smoky flavour on your gas grill easy and convenient.

Direct or Indirect cooking methods...?

The most important barbecuing technique to know is which cooking method, Direct or Indirect, to use for grilling a specific food. The general rule is simple: for foods that take less than 25 minutes to cook, such as kebabs, steaks, chops, vegetables and other small food pieces, use the Direct method.

For foods that require more than 25 minutes of cooking time, such as whole roasts, poultry, racks of ribs and the like, use the Indirect method.

Direct cooking

The Direct method means that the food is cooked directly over the heat source. To ensure that foods cook evenly, turn them only once, halfway through the grilling time.

Direct cooking is also the best technique for searing meats. In addition to creating a wonderful caramelised texture and flavour, searing also adds grill marks to the surface of the meat. To sear meats, place them over Direct heat for 2–5 minutes per side. Remember that smaller pieces of meat require less searing time, and be especially mindful of too much searing on very lean cuts of meat as they can dry out quickly. After searing, finish cooking using the method called for in the recipe.

Direct cooking on a charcoal barbecue

1 Prepare and light the coals as instructed on page 188. Remember, don't begin to barbecue until the coals are covered in a light grey ash. Spread the prepared coals in an even layer across the charcoal grate.

2 Set the cooking grate over the coals and place the food on the cooking grate. Cover with the lid. The food will cook directly over the heat source, as shown in the illustration below.

3 Do not lift the lid during cooking time, except to turn the food once halfway through and to test for doneness.

Direct cooking on a gas barbecue

1 To set up the barbecue for Direct cooking, first preheat with all burners on High. Once the barbecue is up to heat, usually about 10 minutes, adjust all burners to the temperature called for in the recipe.

2 Place the food on the cooking grate and close the lid. Again, the food will be cooked over the heat source, as shown in the illustration below.

3 Do not lift the lid during cooking time, except to turn the food once halfway through and to test for doneness.

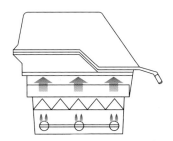

Indirect cooking

Indirect cooking is similar to roasting, but the barbecue adds flavour and texture that you can't get from the oven. The heat rises and reflects off the lid and inside surfaces of the barbecue to cook the food slowly and evenly on all sides. As in a convection oven, there is no need to turn the food over because the heat circulates around the food.

Indirect cooking on a charcoal barbecue

1 Prepare and light the coals as instructed on page 188. Remember, don't begin to barbecue until the coals are covered in a light grey ash. Arrange the hot coals evenly on either side of the charcoal grate. Charcoal/fuel baskets or rails are accessories that keep the coals in place.

2 Place a drip pan in the centre of the charcoal grate between the coals to catch drippings. The drip pan also helps prevent flare-ups when cooking fatty foods

such as duck, goose, or fatty roasts. For longer cooking times, add water to the drip pan to keep the fat and food particles from burning.

3 Set the cooking grate over the coals and place the food on the cooking grate over the drip pan and between the heat zones above the coals.

4 Close the lid and open it only to add coals for longer cooking times, baste the meat or check for doneness.

Indirect cooking on a gas barbecue

1 To set up the barbecue for Indirect cooking, first preheat with all burners on High. Once the barbecue is up to heat, usually about 10 minutes, adjust the burners to the temperature called for in the recipe, turning off the burner(s) directly below the food.

2 Place the food on the cooking grate between the heat zones. (For best results with roasts, poultry or large cuts of meat, use a roasting rack set inside a metal foil pan to catch the drippings.)

3 Close the lid and open it only to baste the meat or check for doneness.

Barbecuing safety

To ensure every barbecue experience is fun and safe, follow these simple rules.

• **Always keep the barbecue at least 10 feet (3 metres) away from any combustible materials** including the house, garage, fences and gates. Do not use the grill indoors or under a covered patio, open garage door, or carport.

• **Keep children and pets away from a hot barbecue at all times.**

• **Do not add lighter fluid to a lit fire.**

• **Make sure the barbecue is sturdy;** do not use if it wobbles, leans or is otherwise unstable. Always stand the barbecue on a firm, level surface.

• **Use heat-resistant barbecue mitts and long-handled tongs** to tend the fire and turn the food.

• **Do not spray oil on a hot cooking grate;** oil the food instead.

• **Do not use water to extinguish a flare-up.** Close the lid (and all vents on a charcoal grill) to reduce the oxygen flow and eliminate flare-ups. If necessary, turn a gas grill off at the source. Keep a fire extinguisher handy in case of a mishap.

• **Do not store propane tanks indoors or in the garage.**

• **When finished barbecuing, close the lid and all vents on a charcoal barbecue; close the lid and turn off all burners and the LP tank or source on a gas grill.** Make sure that hot coals are fully extinguished before leaving the barbecue site.

• **Do not line the bottom of a barbecue or cover the cooking grate with foil.** This obstructs airflow and also collects grease, which can result in flare-ups.

Food safety & preparation

• **Defrost meat, fish and poultry only in the refrigerator, never at room temperature.**

• **Allow meats to come to room temperature before grilling,** but do not do so in a room that is over 70°F/21°C. Do not place raw food in direct sunlight or near a heat source.

• **When using a sauce during grilling, divide it in half and keep one part separate for serving with the finished dish.** Use the other half for basting the meat; do not use this as a sauce for serving. If using a marinade that was used on raw meats, fish or poultry, boil it vigorously for at least 1 full minute before using it as a baste or sauce.

• **Do not place cooked food** on the same platter that the raw food was placed on prior to cooking.

• **Wash all platters, cooking utensils, grilling tools and countertops** that have come into contact with raw meats or fish with hot soapy water. Wash your hands thoroughly after handling raw meats or fish.

• **Chill any leftover cooked food** from the barbecue once it has cooled.

• **Always barbecue ground meats** to at least 160°F/71°C (170°F/77°C for poultry), the temperature for medium (well-done) doneness.

THE BARBECUE TOOL BOX

For best results, use the right tools when barbecuing. Here is a list of some of the essentials:

- **Wide metal spatula**
Used for turning chicken pieces, vegetables and smaller pieces of food.

- **Long-handled grill brush**
Preferably with brass bristles, to keep the grates clean without scratching the porcelain enamel. A steel-bristle brush is best for cleaning cast-iron grates.

- **Basting brush**
Used for basting food with marinade or oil. Best with natural bristles (nylon bristles will melt if they touch the cooking grate) and a long handle.

- **Long-handled tongs**
Used for turning sausages, shellfish, kebabs, etc.

- **Long-handled fork**
Used for lifting cooked roasts and whole poultry from the barbecue. Avoid using a fork for piercing and turning foods, however, as the juices will escape and leave the food dry.

- **Barbecue mitts/oven gloves**
These should be long-sleeved, flame-resistant gloves to protect your hands and forearms.

- **Meat thermometer**
Used for best results every time, a thermometer takes the guess work out of judging food doneness.

- **Timer**
An excellent tool, so you don't have to watch the clock and can continue preparing other parts of the meal while the food is cooking.

- **Foil drip pans**
These keep the base of the barbecue clean and gather fats, juices and bastes that fall from the food during cooking.

- **Skewers**
Excellent for turning pieces of meat, fish or vegetables quickly and easily on the barbecue. Remember to soak wooden skewers, if using them, in cold water for at least 30 minutes before adding the food.

- **Roast holder**
When cooking large cuts of meat and poultry on a gas barbecue, a roast holder placed in a foil pan will help catch the drippings and reduce the chance of flare-ups.

Top: meat thermometer
Centre: roast holder
Bottom: wooden skewers

Maintenance & cleaning tips

Keeping your barbecue clean is the best way to ensure that it gives years of barbecuing pleasure. With simple maintenance and regular cleaning, it will perform better and last longer. These guidelines apply to most barbecues, but be sure to refer to your owner's manual for information specific to your model. The easiest way to keep your charcoal or gas barbecue cooking grates clean on a routine basis is to heat them up and clean them before using, each time. When the barbecue is hot, use a long-handled grill brush or crumpled foil to remove the loosened particles from the cooking grates. The heat virtually 'sterilises' the cooking grates, and brushing them while hot eliminates any residual flavours, fats or food particles. Before storing the barbecue for a long period, or until the next time you use it regularly, give it a thorough all-over cleaning.

Charcoal barbecues

Cooking grates – after each use, remove food particles using a brass-bristle brush or crumpled-up foil. As needed, remove the cooking grates and wash them with warm, soapy water or, for extreme build-up, gently use a soap-embedded, fine steel wool pad.

Inside the lid – wash with a soft cloth soaked in warm, soapy water (see note and caution below).

Outside surfaces – periodically wash with warm, soapy water. You can use a non-toxic glass cleaner to return some of the shine to the porcelain enamel. For stainless steel surfaces, use a soft cloth and a stainless steel cleaner.

Vents and ash catcher – for the ash catcher, first throw away cold ashes, then wash in mild, soapy water. Use the same for cleaning the vents.

Smoke stains – smoke stains may appear on the edges of the lid or around the vents. They may look like rust as they are reddish-brown or black in colour. Use a soapy scrub pad very gently to remove the stains.

NOTE: If it looks like paint is peeling off the inside of your lid, don't worry. It is not paint. The flakes you see are just accumulated cooking vapours that have turned into carbon. They are not harmful, but you can get rid of them by brushing the lid with a brass bristle brush or a crumpled piece of aluminium foil. Once you have cleaned the lid after cooking, you can wipe the inside of the lid with a paper towel while the grill is still warm (not hot) to minimise further build-up. CAUTION: Do not use oven cleaner, abrasive cleaners (kitchen cleaners), cleaners that contain citrus products or abrasive cleaning pads on any part of your barbecue.

Gas barbecues

Burner tents/Flavorizer® bars – remove debris periodically using a brass-bristle brush. As needed, remove the bars and wash with warm soapy water. Do not use oven cleaner, abrasive cleaners, cleaners that contain citrus products or abrasive cleaning pads on any part of your barbecue.

Bottom drip tray – remove excess grease that has collected in the bottom tray and replace the aluminium liner. Use a plastic putty knife to scrape off excess accumulation, then wash with warm, soapy water.

Inside the lid – wash with a soft cloth soaked in warm, soapy water (see note and caution below left).

Outside surfaces – periodically wash with warm, soapy water. You can use a non-toxic glass cleaner to return some of the shine to the porcelain enamel. For stainless steel surfaces, use a soft cloth and a stainless steel cleaner.

Cooking grates – Burn off any residue by simply turning the grill on High until the smoke stops, then brush the cooking grates with a brass-bristle brush. (Note: For cast-iron cooking grates use a steel brush.)

Gas tank – check for gas leaks each time you disconnect and reconnect the fitting on the tank. Do not use an open flame to check for leaks, and be sure there are no open flames or sparks in the area before checking. Using a soap-and-water solution, turn on the gas at the source and gently wipe the connections and hoses – bubbles indicate a leak. Regularly check the hose for cracks, abrasions or cuts. Always check the gas tank yourself, even if it was dealer- or store-installed. Make sure the gas is always turned off at the source when the barbecue is not in use.

> NOTE: Always store the tank (and spare, if you have one) outdoors, never inside. If the barbecue is stored indoors, disconnect the gas supply and store the tank outdoors.

Barbecuing tips for success

The following checklist will prove valuable in helping you prepare for stress-free barbecuing.

Always make sure the barbecue is up to temperature before beginning to cook anything. Remember that the charcoal should have a light grey ash on it for a good hot fire, which takes between 25 and 30 minutes. Use a chimney starter for best results.

Keep extra coals ready for roasts and large cuts of meat that require adding coals to the fire during the barbecuing time.

Always barbecue with the lid down.

DON'T PEEK! Turn food only once, halfway through cooking time, and leave the lid closed the rest of the time. Heat escapes each time the lid is opened, resulting in longer cooking times.

Keep air vents on a charcoal barbecue open to help air circulate and keep the fire going.

Avoid using a fork to turn meats – use a spatula or tongs instead to ensure that the juices do not run out.

Resist brushing marinades, glazes or basting sauces that have a high sugar content, on the food, until the last 15–20 minutes of barbecuing time.

Plan ahead. Direct, Indirect or both? If a recipe calls for searing the food over Direct heat and then finishing over Indirect heat, set up your barbecue for an Indirect fire first. Sear the food directly over the coals, and then move your food over to Indirect heat to finish.

To minimize flare-ups, trim excess fat from meats, leaving no more than a 5mm/¼ inch thick layer.

Soak wooden skewers (or any other type of skewer that burns easily), in cold water for at least 30 minutes before putting the food on them.

Barbecue guides

The following thicknesses, weights and barbecue times are meant to be general guidelines rather than firm rules and you may notice that recipe times vary in comparison. When following a recipe, always follow the specific instructions. Cooking times are affected by wind, outside temperature and desired degree of doneness. However, there are two general rules of thumb to keep in mind:

• Barbecue steaks, fish fillets, boneless chicken pieces and vegetables using the Direct method for the times given on the chart, or to the desired doneness, turning once halfway through cooking.

• Barbecue joints, whole poultry, roasts, whole fish and thicker cuts of meat using the Indirect method for the time given on the chart, or until the meat has reached the indicated internal temperature.

All cooking times/temperatures on the charts are for medium doneness.

Let joints, chops, steaks, and larger cuts of meat and poultry rest for 5–10 minutes before carving or serving. The internal temperature of the meat will rise to a perfect medium doneness during this time, and the juices will settle back into the meat for maximum barbecue flavour.

KEY TO METHOD OF COOKING

In the following fish, poultry, meat and vegetable charts on pages 199–204, the approximate cooking time is followed by the barbecue method, as below:

DM	Direct Medium heat
DH	Direct High heat
DL	Direct Low heat
IM	Indirect Medium heat
IH	Indirect High heat

Fish and shellfish guide

Fish for the barbecue falls into three categories: fish fillets, whole fish and shellfish. Generally, fish fillets, kebabs and shellfish should be barbecued over Direct heat and large whole fish over Indirect heat for the times indicated. Use heavy-duty tin foil under any fish that is quite flaky when cooked, or whole fillets of fish, such as a side of salmon. Place the fish on the foil and bring it around the sides of the fish like a shallow tray. Fish barbecued in this way should not be turned during cooking.

Most fish can be cooked on the barbecue but, for a true barbecue flavour and appearance, some varieties will work better than others. Fish such as cod and haddock are impossible to turn and should be supported by heavy-duty tin foil because they flake and fall apart easily. While they can be cooked in this fashion, some of the charred flavour and the blackened grill marks associated with barbecuing or grilling are sacrificed.

Remember, that unless you are using a very firm-fleshed fish like monkfish or tuna, it can break up unless it's supported by its own skin and bones. Hence, a lot of fish is cooked whole, but even some of these need to be treated with care or they can stick and break on the cooking grate. Always oil the fish well before grilling. A general rule for grilling fish is 4–5 minutes per 1.5cm–$\frac{1}{2}$ inch thickness and 8–10 minutes per 2.5cm/1 inch thickness. To check when a fillet is perfectly cooked (usually at the point when the centre is just changing from translucent to opaque), cut it open to see. The flesh will be firm and will just give slightly when ready.

Wherever possible, grill shellfish with the shells on to retain their juices. Mussels and clams can be cooked in a pan over Direct heat or wrapped in foil parcels as our recipes suggest on pages 56 and 59. It is important to remember that if any shells don't open they must be discarded.

type of fish/shellfish	thickness or weight	approx cooking time	
fish fillet or steak	1.5cm/$\frac{1}{2}$ inch thick	3–5 mins	DH
	2cm/$\frac{3}{4}$ inch thick	5–10 mins	DH
	2.5cm/1 inch thick	10–12 mins	DH
fish kebab	2.5cm/1 inch thick	8–10 mins	DM
fish, whole	450g/1lb		
	(5–6.5cm/2–2$\frac{1}{2}$ inches thick)	15–20 mins	IM
	450–900g/1–2lb	20–30 mins	IM
	900g–1.75kg/2–4lb	30–45 mins	IM
crab	approx. 1.25kg/2$\frac{1}{2}$lb	10–12 mins	DM
lobster, split lengthwise	approx. 900g/2lb	8–10 mins	DM
lobster tail	225–300g/8–10oz	8–12 mins	DM
prawn with shell	medium	4–5 mins	DH
	large	5–6 mins	DH
	extra large	6–8 mins	DH
prawn without shell (tiger/langoustine)	about 1–2 mins less than the above timings		DH
scallop without shell	2.5–5cm/1–2 inches diameter	3–6 mins	DH
clam	medium	8–10 mins	DH
	(discard any that do not open)		
oyster	small	3–6 mins	DH
mussel	medium	5–6 mins	DH
	(discard any that do not open)		

Poultry guide

When it comes to poultry, we are spoiled for choice. There are handy packed portions or whole oven-ready birds ranging from corn-fed, free range to organic. Think about how you plan to prepare and cook your chicken before buying. If you intend to marinate with strong flavours or spices you can safely choose a cheaper breed or cut. Less

aromatic treatments or simple plain grilling call for a better quality bird. Chicken tastes best when grilled with it's skin still on. It can, of course, be grilled without the skin but, because most of the fat lies just underneath, removing it will mean that the chicken will need extra oil or marinade to keep it moist and prevent it from drying out.

Whole birds and poultry pieces

Cook pieces bone side down for the given time or until no longer pink in the centre. Cook whole birds breast side up. Chicken pieces with the skin on should be cooked skin side up to allow the juices to penetrate the meat. The skin can then be removed before serving for a leaner finished dish. If you plan to serve the pieces with the skin on, you can quickly sear, skin side down, for about 2 minutes, then turn over and finish grilling skin side up. Duck breasts should be barbecued skin side down first, then turned over once halfway through cooking. To release the fat slowly during cooking, score the duck skin in a diamond pattern, being sure not to cut into the meat. Whole birds like turkey and goose should be put on a rack in a roasting tin when cooking on a gas barbecue.

Boneless chicken and turkey

Place the boneless chicken or turkey pieces on the cooking grate and barbecue over Direct heat. All cooking times are for well done meat (the meat should no longer be pink in the centre and the juices should run clear).

type of poultry	thickness or weight	approx cooking time	
chicken, whole	1.5–2.25kg/3½–5lb	1–1½ hours	IM
chicken, half, bone-in	675–800g/1¼–1½lb	1–1¼ hours	IM
chicken breast, boneless and skinless	175g/6oz	8–12 mins	DM
chicken pieces, breast or wing, bone-in	approx. 225g/8oz	30–40 mins	IM
chicken pieces, leg or thigh, bone-in	100–175g/4–6oz	40–50 mins	IM
chicken thigh, boneless and skinless	100g/4oz	8–10 mins	DM
chicken kebab	2.5cm/1 inch cube	6–8 mins	DM
chicken burger	2cm/¾ inch thick	10–12 mins	DM
poussin, whole	350g–450g/12oz–1lb	40–50 mins	IM
turkey, whole, unstuffed	4.5–5kg/10–11lb 5.5–6.5 kg/12–14lb 6.75–7.5kg/15–17lb 8–10kg/18–22lb (general guideline: 11–13 mins per 450g/1lb)	1¾–2½ hours 2¼–3 hours 2¾–3¾ hours 3½–4 hours	IM IM IM IM
turkey breast, bone-in	1.5 kg/4–5lb	1–1½ hours	IM
turkey drumstick, bone-in	450–675g/½–1½lb	¾–1¼ hours	IM
turkey breast escalope	5mm–1cm/¼–½ inch thick	4–6 mins	DM
turkey breast kebab	2.5cm/1 inch cube	6–8 mins	DM
turkey breast, boneless	1.75kg/4lb	1 hour	DM
duck, whole	1.75–2.75kg/4–6lb	1½–2 hours	IM
duck breast, boneless	250–300g/9–10oz (approx 1.5cm–¾ inch thick)	12–14 mins	DL
goose, whole	4.5–6.5kg/10–12lb	3 hours	IM

safe cooking temperature chart
cook whole poultry to 180°F/82°C
cook ground poultry to 165°/74°C
cook chicken breasts to 170°F/77°C
cook duck and goose to 180°F/82°C

Meat guide

If possible, buy your steaks from a butcher where you can ask for them to be cut to a certain thickness which will allow the grilling guides to be followed as closely as possible. With experience, you will be able to tell exactly at what point to remove the meat from the grill, whether your taste is for rare or well done. If you are unsure whether a piece of meat is cooked through, don't cut into your meat! That can cause juices and flavour to escape and can dry out your food, too. Simply insert an instant-read thermometer into the centre of the meat to check for your desired doneness.

Beef & veal

All times are based on medium doneness (cook a little longer for well done); turn meat once halfway through cooking time. Always let the meat rest, covered with aluminium foil, for 5–10 minutes after removing from the grill. This not only allows the juices to settle for full flavour, but the meat continues cooking during this time and the internal temperature rises, giving the food perfect medium doneness. Steaks should be grilled using the Direct method. For roasts or large cuts of meat, grill using the Indirect method for the time given.

type of beef/veal	thickness or weight	approx cooking time
steak: **sirloin, rib or T-bone**	2.5cm/1 inch thick 4cm/1½ inches thick (sear 10 mins DH, then 6–8 mins IM) 5cm/2 inches thick (sear 10 mins DH, then 10–14 mins IM)	10–12 mins DM 16–18 mins DH/IM 20–24 mins DH/IM
thick rump tip or rump steak	450–900g/1–2lb	12–15 mins DM
brisket	2.25–2.75kg/5–6lb	2½–3 hours IM
boneless sirloin roast	1.75–2.75kg/4–6lb	1–1½ hours IM
hamburger	2cm/¾ inch thick	8–10 mins DM
veal chop	2.5cm/1 inch thick	10–12 mins DM

safe cooking temperature chart
cook beef roasts and steaks to
145°F/62°C for medium rare
(160°F/71°C for medium)
cook ground beef to at least 160°F/71°C

Lamb

Grill lamb chops using the Direct method. All times are based on medium doneness (cook a little longer for well done and a little less for medium rare); turn meat once halfway through cooking time. Let the meat rest, covered with aluminium foil, for 5–10 minutes after removing from the grill. The meat continues cooking during this time and the internal temperature rises, giving the food a perfect medium doneness. For roasts or large cuts of meat, grill using the Indirect method for the time given.

type of lamb	thickness or weight	approx cooking time	
chop: loin, rib or chump	2.5cm/1 inch thick	8–12 mins	DM
leg of lamb steak	2.5cm/1 inch thick	10–12 mins	DM
rack of lamb	675g/1½lb	25–35 mins	DM
leg of lamb, boneless/rolled	2.25–2.75kg/6–7lb	2½ hours	IM

safe cooking temperature chart
cook lamb to 145°F/62°C for medium rare
(160°F/71°C for medium)
cook minced lamb to 160°F/71°C

Pork

Grill pork chops using the Direct method when 2–2.5cm/³⁄₄–1 inch in thickness and the Indirect method/Medium heat for thicker chops. All times are based on medium doneness (pork should not be pink in the centre). Turn meat once halfway during grilling time. Let the meat rest, covered with aluminium foil, for 5–10 minutes after removing from the grill. The meat continues cooking during this time and the internal temperature rises, giving the food a perfect medium doneness. For pork roasts, follow the method for beef or lamb. Pork sausages should be cooked using the Indirect method being careful of flare-ups if they are fatty. They should be cooked well and not be pink in the centre.

type of pork	thickness or weight	approx cooking time	
chop: rib, loin or shoulder	2cm/³⁄₄ inch thick 3cm/1¼ inches thick	10–15 mins DM 14–18 mins DH/IM (sear 8 mins DH, then 6–10 mins IM)	
loin roast	1.5–2.25kg/3–5lb	1¼–1¾ hours	IM
spareribs	1.5–1.75/3–4lb	1½–2 hours	IM
loin chop, boneless	2cm/³⁄₄ inch thick	10–12 mins	DM
tenderloin (pork steak)	350–450g/12oz–1lb	25–30 mins	IM
sausage		25–30 mins	IM

safe cooking temperature chart
cook all pork to 160°F/71°C

Vegetable guide

Most vegetables can be cooked on the barbecue with great results. Large vegetables, such as red and green peppers or onions, can be barbecued as they come, placed directly on the cooking grate and then turned with tongs. Smaller cuts of vegetables, or small vegetables like mushrooms, are best skewered to make turning easier and quicker. Vegetables should be lightly brushed with olive oil before grilling to prevent them from sticking to the cooking grate. Unless otherwise specified, all vegetables should be turned once halfway through the cooking time. Cooking times indicated in the chart are for crisp, tender vegetables.

type of vegetable	approx cooking time	
artichoke, globe, whole	steam 20–25 mins; cut in half and grill 8–10 mins	DM
asparagus, whole, trimmed	6–8 mins	DM
aubergine, 1cm/½ inch slices	8–10 mins	DM
halved	12–15 mins	DM
corn, husked	10–12 mins	DM
in husk	25–30 mins	DM
courgettes, 1cm/½ inch slices	6–8 mins	DM
halved	6–10 mins	DM
fennel, 5mm/¼ inch slices	10–12 mins	DM
garlic, whole	45–60 mins	IM
leek, whole	14–16 mins	DM
mushroom: shiitake or button	8–10 mins	DM
portobello	12–15 mins	DM
onion, whole (do not peel)	45–50 mins	IM
peeled and halved	35–40 mins	IM
1cm/½ inch slices	8–12 mins	DM
spring onion, whole, trimmed	3–4 mins	DM
pepper, whole	10–12 mins	DM
halved or quartered	6–8 mins	DM
potato, whole	45–60 mins	IM
1cm/½ inch slices	14–16 mins	DM
new, halved	20–25 mins	DM
squash: acorn 450g/1lb	40–45 mins	IM
butternut 900g/2lb	50–55 mins	IM
spaghetti 1.5kg/3lb	1¼–1½ hours	IM
sweet potato, 5mm/¼ inch slices	8–10 mins	DM
tomato, halved	6–8 mins	DM
1cm/½ inch slices	2–4 mins	DM
whole	8–10 mins	DM
cherry, whole	2–4 mins	DM
plum, halved	6–8 mins	DM

Index

Acknowledgements

MQ Publications would like to thank the following for their kind permission to reproduce the photographs :

Alamy 49t
Andalucia Slide Library / Michelle Chaplow 10tc, 26bl
Anthony Blake Picture Library 8, 29bl, 37bl, 55bl, 65bl, 78bl, 102tc, 131bl, 135bl, 138bl
Corbis / Owen Franken 102b, 116bl, 123tr, 169bl; Ray Juno 114t, 162tr
Francesca Yorke 10b, 144br
Garden Picture Library / Mayer 140b; Michel Viaro 75b
Getty Images / Colin Patterson 68b
Mel Yates 24tl, 24tr, 32t
MQP/ Janine Hosegood 140tl; 172b
The Travel Library / R. Richardson 24b
Robert Harding Picture Library 10tr, 60t
Stock Food 31bl, 41bl, 140tc
Weber-Stephen Products Co. 186tr; 189bl; 191br; 194; 195t; 195c; 202 / Chris Alack 24tc; 56bl; 68tc, tr; 81; 87; 102tl; 129; 140tr; 142; 172tl, tc; 186tl, tc, b; 192; 195br; 196; 200 / Ken Field all recipe photography / Olivier Maynard 48bl; 172tr

Every effort has been made to trace the copyright holders. MQ Publications apologises for unintentional omissions however, and would be pleased in such cases to add an acknowledgment in future editions.